The Writer's Handbook
Guide to Travel Writing

Barry Turner has worked on both sides of publishing, as an editor and marketing director and as an author. He started his career as a journalist with *The Observer* before moving on to television and radio. He has written over twenty books including *A Place in the Country*, which inspired a television series, and a bestselling biography of the actor Richard Burton.

His recent work includes a radio play, travel articles, serialising books for *The Times*, editing the magazine *Country* and writing a one-man show based on the life of the legendary theatre critic, James Agate. Barry has just published *Countdown to Victory*, a book about the last months of World War II. He has been editor of *The Writer's Handbook* for eighteen years, and editor of *The Statesman's Yearbook* for seven.

Also edited by Barry Turner
in *The Writer's Handbook* series

The Writer's Handbook Guide to Writing for Children

Featuring articles and interviews with established authors and experts in the trade, this book explores the key to success in writing for children and offers all the necessary advice for newcomers to this expanding market.

The Writer's Handbook Guide to Crime Writing

Drawing on a wide range of expertise, including top crime writers, agents, publishers and booksellers, this book looks at how to write a successful crime novel and get it published.

The Writer's Handbook Guide to Writing for Stage and Screen

There are increasing opportunities for new writers of plays, be it for stage, screen or radio – but also increasing demands. This highly practical and informative book looks at how to get started, and how to become a successful playwright in any area.

The Writer's Handbook 2005

The eighteenth edition of the bestselling guide to all markets for creative writing. Completely revised and updated, this is an indispensable companion for everyone in the writing profession. Offering a cornucopia of advice, information, contacts, hints and discussion, this practical, straightforward guide provides full details on the key markets.

The Writer's Handbook
Guide to Travel Writing

edited by

BARRY TURNER

MACMILLAN

First published 2004 by Macmillan
an imprint of Pan Macmillan Ltd
Pan Macmillan, 20 New Wharf Road, London N1 9RR
Basingstoke and Oxford
Associated companies throughout the world
www.panmacmillan.com

ISBN 1 4050 4178 1

Copyright © Macmillan Publishers Ltd 2004

Editorial research Jill Fenner and Daniel Smith

The right of Barry Turner to be identified as the
editor of this work has been asserted by him in accordance
with the Copyright, Designs and Patents Act 1988.

All rights reserved. No part of this publication may be
reproduced, stored in or introduced into a retrieval system, or
transmitted, in any form, or by any means (electronic, mechanical,
photocopying, recording or otherwise) without the prior written
permission of the publisher. Any person who does any unauthorized
act in relation to this publication may be liable to criminal
prosecution and civil claims for damages.

1 3 5 7 9 8 6 4 2

Inclusion in *The Writer's Handbook Guide to Travel Writing*
is entirely at the editor's discretion. Macmillan Publishers Ltd
makes no recommendation whatsoever by the inclusion or
omission of any agency, publisher or organisation.

While every effort has been made to ensure all of the information
contained in this publication is correct and accurate, the publisher cannot
accept any responsibility for any omissions or errors that may
occur or for any consequences arising there from.

A CIP catalogue record for this book is available from
the British Library.

Typeset by Intypelibra, London
Printed and bound in Great Britain by
Mackays of Chatham plc, Chatham, Kent

This book is sold subject to the condition that it shall not,
by way of trade or otherwise, be lent, re-sold, hired out,
or otherwise circulated without the publisher's prior consent
in any form of binding or cover other than that in which
it is published and without a similar condition including this
condition being imposed on the subsequent purchaser.

All Pan Macmillan titles are available from www.panmacmillan.com
or from Macmillan Direct on 01256 302699

Contents

LISTINGS

Introduction to Travel Writing

Author Mick Sinclair surveys the
market for travel writing

Exploring far-flung countries, discovering exotic cities, sampling the world's finest hotels and restaurants, and embarking on every kind of adventure imaginable – travel writing for a living is the stuff dreams are made of. Predictably, making the dream a reality is a bit more down to earth and begins with the hardest thing a travel writer ever has to do: find an opening.

Newspapers

On any weekend, the travel sections of national newspapers are crammed with travel articles and this is a logical place to try your hand at getting published. Bear in mind the amount of space is dictated by advertising and the middle of a downturn is not the best time to be competing with established and regular contributors. Nonetheless, if your piece manages to be what is required, there is no reason why it will not be used, provided it is sufficiently well written and suits the style of the paper.

Never forget that travel editors are besieged with speculative copy, most of which begins with the author's journey to the airport and is in the bin before they reach take-off speed. Finding a personal and offbeat take on somewhere familiar and a lively start: 'When the stench of the sewer hit my nostrils I knew I'd arrived in . . .' will have more chance of enticing the editor to read beyond the first sentence than vaguely offering an article 'about Paris' or 'my Mediterranean cruise'.

Read the contributors' guidelines which are usually posted on the newspaper's website and send your copy by email or post as suggested. Even if the editor likes your piece he or she will not clear the decks to use it, so be prepared for a long wait. It is not unusual to wait a year before a free slot comes up, so don't provide anything that may quickly become dated. It's entirely reasonable to check how things stand with an email to the relevant person (use an actual name wherever possible), but don't do this too often: you can't pester your way into publication.

Because travel editors have an annoying tendency to travel, it's likely you'll be communicating with the editor's assistant and this is a relationship worth cultivating, even if it sometimes seems one of constant rejection. If you are repeatedly ignored (not necessarily a reflection on your work), take the hint and try placing your piece elsewhere.

Fact-based features, such as those focusing on recommended hotels or restaurants are usually specifically commissioned from established writers and require particular skills, not least the ability to make dozens of near-identical establishments sound highly individual. However, if this type of work is what you want, keep compiling and suggesting lists: luxurious island hotels, romantic getaways, great weekend breaks and the like have limitless appeal and consequently limitless numbers of people compiling them. The less obvious and more quirky might be more successful: great gourmet restaurants adjacent to theme parks, ten luxury hotels overlooking cemeteries, five spots for city centre fishing – if only to demonstrate that you have a creative mind and an imaginative take on travel.

Away from the nationals, most leading regional newspapers have travel slots and generally the same rules apply. These are, of course, less prestigious places for your byline than a national but nonetheless will help to build up a portfolio of published pieces. Your local free sheet will probably be happy to take anything provided it has a strong local focus: 'neighbourhood travel writer triumphs in Asian sandcastle building contest', for example, but expect little remuneration and zero kudos.

Magazines

Many of the same techniques for approaching newspapers apply to magazines, be they glossy monthlies or free unglossy weeklies, though there are some important caveats. Be very aware of the magazine's target readership, which is more narrowly defined than that of newspapers. Obvious (and perhaps sexist and ageist) it may be, but a publication aimed at middle-aged women is unlikely to want something on rave weekends in Ibiza (unless perhaps from a lock-up-your-daughters perspective); likewise a motoring-based magazine may not be impressed with a travel piece devoted to praising a region's public transport system. Tailor your writing to the readers' interests without, of course, becoming patronising.

In monthlies, space is much more limited than with newspapers and, unless the publication specialises in travel, only ten or so travel articles a year are likely to be run; most of these commissioned from regular writers. Offer ideas rather than submitting speculative copy and remember that each issue is planned many months in advance: old hands typically spend their summers composing 'Where To Spend Christmas' stories. However, where a past event has an impact on travel it would be foolish not to deal with it. If writing about Bali, for example, it would be essential to

3

mention the 2002 bombings, particularly at a time when safety concerns are uppermost in readers' minds.

Free weekly magazines, commonly found in major cities, can be a good place to hone your style (if you can provide original photos, too, then so much the better) and some pay relatively decently, but few carry any gravitas in the wider travel-writing world.

Overseas newspapers and magazines

Think globally: you are a travel writer, after all. Your work can find an outlet in newspapers and magazines all over the world and, thanks to the internet and email, they are as easy to read (and contact) as their UK counterparts. The biggest circulations and consequently the best paying tend to be in the USA; start with the bestselling and work down. But remember that Americans are likely to want emphasis on top-of-the-range restaurants and accommodation and assurances on decent services.

Guidebooks

Travel guide publishers commonly commission guidebooks as a series rather than as individual titles and will be impressed as much with a would-be author's awareness of the series, its overall tone and target readership, as by detailed knowledge of a destination.

Having explored the publisher's website, follow the 'author guidelines' and proceed accordingly. Send relevant details and experience (alas, having been on holiday many times does not count as relevant experience) and a CV, but only provide the latter if asked to or if it's directly relevant. Most publishers will be looking for evidence of a person being able to work and organise himself independently and, above all, someone who will not wilt when confronted with a deadline.

With marketing arranged well in advance and publication dates set in stone, the writer absolutely must be able to deliver on time, which could mean producing 30,000 quality words in six weeks or 100,000 inside four months. Writers must also be willing and able to revise where necessary; even the most experienced author spends weeks revising drafts until every word earns its place on the page. Do all this well and you are likely to be offered another title from the same publishers, even if it's somewhere you're never been before, just because they believe you can do it.

Adventure books

Despite the success of Bill Bryson and Peter Mayle, publishers unfailingly inform authors contemplating similar undertakings – first-hand accounts of a potentially life-changing journey through landscapes populated by all manner of exotic characters – that such books do not sell.

Unfortunately, they are right most of the time, although there are unknowns who do unexpectedly well, such as Chris Stewart with *Driving Over Lemons*. Without a track record, however, authors will need to have had the experience and written most of the book before touting the idea to a publisher and should be particularly careful to find a suitable niche: a year of mine-clearing in Cambodia might have little appeal to a major publisher but may tickle the fancy of a small house specialising in developing-nation issues.

If you think your adventure has a book in it, prove it to yourself before trying to convince a publisher. Anecdotes that thrill a captive bar audience can suddenly seem very shallow when written down and extended to chapter length. Write a detailed outline (to show the idea will work in book form), sample chapters (to show you can actually write) and create enough suspense to make the publisher (as well as, eventually, the reader) want to turn the page to find out what happened next.

Having said that, writers hoping to break into travel authorship by recounting a thrill-a-minute tale of death-defying adventure will probably find swimming the Atlantic with a pack of sharks or crossing Antarctica on a toboggan to be much easier than convincing a publisher to commission an account of the exploit. If you convince the publisher a TV tie-in is in the offing, however, it may be a very different matter.

Off the beaten track

Just as successful travel writing often means ignoring the obvious and seeking out unusual angles, there are many off-the-beaten-track routes into the field.

Contract publishers produce magazines on behalf of corporate clients of all kinds, from department stores and car manufacturers to fitness clubs and digital TV providers. Their readerships are perceived as leading affluent lifestyles in which travel plays an important part, whether for pleasure or business, and this is reflected in the publication's content. The relatively low readership of such titles may mean you will not become a household name, but payments are generally quite good, largely due to the magazine's high advertising rates.

The courtesy magazines of airlines, cruise lines, ferry boats and even some rail operators, all have a natural interest in travel articles related to their routes. As well as offering general ideas, keep an ear to the ground, or perhaps an eye on the skies, for news of any new routes being applied for by particular companies; have a suitable suggestion ready for the editor for when the routes become reality.

Rather obviously, the travel brochures of tour companies need to be written by somebody. Global brands tend to have their own people producing the all-too-predictable copy; approaching smaller independents specialising in a particular region or speciality (*see* 'Becoming an expert', *below*) may be more rewarding if you can match your interests to theirs.

Local and regional tourist offices often produce their own brochures, leaflets and items of special interest, all of which need a competent person to write them; most also have website pages to fill. Suggest something over and above their usual fare: woodland walks, perhaps, or local literary nooks, that can promote a region without falling into tourist office clichés. Local museums, too, are potential sources for work, even if they are likely to be poor payers.

Are you qualified?

Despite the growing popularity of media studies, no university offers a degree course in travel writing. In any case, hard-nosed editors tend not to be impressed by anybody waving academic qualifications around if there is no evidence they can actually provide the goods. That said, some qualifications are handy and they are not always the ones you might first think of.

Any vocational study in a travel-related field, such as hotel management or cookery, might bring revealing insider's insights when covering accommodation or dining options. A grounding in geography could prove worthwhile when superlatives alone cannot do justice to a landscape.

While languages are less essential than most people imagine, it's obviously a help to understand Japanese if writing about Japan.

7

Perhaps less obviously French would be very useful in parts of Africa, Canada and the Caribbean, and Spanish handy for a large chunk of the world.

Becoming an expert

Becoming an 'expert' on a region is not as difficult as it might sound. Relatively in-depth knowledge of, say, Thailand, may be brought about by a modicum of background reading on anything from history and economics to religion, political issues and cultural matters, and by keeping abreast of the country's English-language newspapers (available online). This will make you better informed than the jobbing travel writer whose knowledge of the south-east Asian country might begin and end with beaches, fake goods and spicy food.

The instant your work takes a step (even a tiny step) beyond the usual boundaries readers and editors alike will sit up and take notice. Think of yourself as a foreign correspondent with your finger on the country's pulse. Of course, the more countries whose pulses you have a finger on, the better.

Finding a niche

Becoming the acknowledged first port of call when information is needed on, for example, travelling with kids, watching wildlife, the haunts of the rich and famous, celebrity retreats, or budget biking holidays, can be rewarding. Niches are sometimes found by accident. It's not unknown, for example, for a writer who adds a paragraph about football grounds to an article about Italy to find himself being approached to write a detailed book on the subject, even if he is far too professional to admit he doesn't actually like the game.

Being recognised as having a specialist niche is a fine and potentially lucrative thing, but bear in mind typecasting can apply to writers as much as to actors. Spending years convincing the world that you really are the leading authority on Scandinavian youth hostels is not the best preparation for subsequently suggesting that you are the best person to tackle that all-expenses-paid trip to the finest restaurants of Paris, however much it might be true.

Rounding up the usual clichés

Whether creating copy to order or knocking up something to offer speculatively, there are some general rules to be considered, if not always obeyed. There was a time when nearly all travel writing was known not for informed commentary on the subject matter but for the number of clichés that could be strung together in describing a place where markets are 'colourful', where waterfalls always 'cascade' and where sunsets are unfailingly 'glorious'.

Readers and publishers alike are nowadays alert to the above and to the use of 'paradise' or 'Mecca' to describe anything above average and 'contrasts' (perhaps the one thing every place on earth can claim) being employed in almost any context. Writers should also watch out for lazily describing ethnic areas as 'vibrant', praising a restaurant's 'sinful' desserts, and recommending a place for its 'pulsating' night life. Admittedly some clichés are unavoidable because the cliché is true; some apparently, since copy-editors seem surprisingly keen to insert them, are desirable.

Having avoided clichés, certain recurring phrases and other travel-writing quirks can be mulled over. What exactly is 'authentic' cuisine? Why does anybody need to know exactly how many rooms a hotel has? Do architects actually 'build' buildings or do they really only 'design' them? Do buildings date from when they were started, finished or formally opened: should San Francisco's Grace Cathedral, for example, be dated as 1910 (cornerstone laid), 1928 (construction begins) or 1964 (consecration)?

Be consistent and accurate. If an editor phones with a query, be ready not only to answer it but to justify what you've written, especially if it contradicts what everybody else says.

Freebies

For beginners, getting a freebie, an escorted, all-expenses-paid trip, is as hard as getting published. Unless your interests really do begin and end with freeloading, don't even think about approaching travel companies, airlines, hotels or anyone else without at least proof of relevant commissions and the near-certainty that your writing will greatly enhance their customer numbers.

There are exceptions, such as orchestrated affairs when selected hacks, likely to be chosen for their susceptibility to gin-and-tonic, are chaperoned throughout and expected to repay the hospitality with reams of uncritical praise, but the freebie of popular imagination barely exists in the real, accounts-conscious world of travel and is generally beyond the grasp of the novice.

Local hotel and restaurant owners are unlikely to be falling over themselves to be mentioned in anything other than specialist publications or by local reviewers. Mainstream guidebooks typically include hundreds of hotels and dining places, leaving little incentive for a particular establishment to offer complimentary or even discounted rates to travel writers.

Some countries, notably the USA, are helpful to the media. But many others appear to have re-written an old adage to read 'any publicity is potentially bad publicity' and treat travel writers accordingly. Remember, too, that any complimentary or discounted travel that is on offer is liable to involve winter in Scandinavia, the hurricane season in the Caribbean, or the monsoon season in Asia, all staples of the travel writer's yearly itinerary.

Paved with gold

Most travel writers earn a living, but not a great one, and do so by spending more of their time sitting at a desk actually putting words together than cavorting around a destination.

Sadly, remuneration tends not to be excessive. For newspaper and magazine articles, the payment will almost certainly be the organ's minimum rate per word regardless of how long the writer was away. Some guidebook publishers pay a royalty, which is preferable in most instances though sales are, obviously, directly proportional to the popularity of the destination: even the definitive *Backpacking in Tristan da Cunha* will not make its author rich. The majority of guide publishers pay a fee per word akin to that of a moderately-paying magazine.

For a new title, fee-paying book publishers usually (but not always) add an amount to the basic fee to cover 'expenses' which is normally defined (if it is defined at all) as costs of flights and accommodation with very little extra for sustenance, despite the expectation of extensive restaurant recommendations, and certainly nothing for time spent away from home working perhaps seven days a week and twelve hours a day. Complain about this to the publisher and the words 'free' and 'holiday' will be heard. Royalty-paying guide publishers commonly offer nothing more than an advance on the royalty.

A foot in the door

However much travel writers complain (and they do complain) about their lot, the pleasures always outweigh the hardships. Travel writing exceptionally rewards its practitioners with more exotic experiences, more meetings with memorable people and more insights into the workings of the world in a year than most people encounter in a lifetime.

Admittedly, the journey into travel writing is a difficult one with no positive result guaranteed. Embark on it as you would on a trip: with your eyes wide open, ready for any possibility, and always open to new ideas. It might be a long, hard slog, but ultimately the destination will be reached and it may turn out to be an even more splendid one than you dared imagine.

Mick Sinclair's latest book is Cities of the Imagination: San Francisco, *published by Signal Books. He has also authored guides for AA Publishing, Duncan-Petersen, New Holland, Thomas Cook and Rough Guides. His travel writing has appeared in newspapers and magazines throughout the world.*

Spare Me the Holiday Snaps

Cath Urquhart, Travel Editor of The Times,
talks to Adam Hopkins

ADAM HOPKINS: You must have a good view of what your readers like, what appeals to them; and what doesn't.

CATH URQUHART: We hope we do. We take the view at *The Times* that our readers are well educated, they're curious about the world. They are, to use marketing jargon, probably ABC, reasonably high earners, and range from captains of industry to just well educated and professional people. Many of them are metropolitan; we sell a lot of copies in London and the south-east so we bear that in mind.

AH: You could say that about other broadsheets. Is it fair to lump you all together?

CU: To a certain extent. We are not as right-wing as the *Telegraph* and not as left-wing as the *Guardian*, we like to say we are a bit of a broad church.

AH: But when it comes to travel what do you think appeals to your readers? What makes for a good article?

CU: OK. Remember that good journalism is first and foremost about people. That's true of a news story or a feature and it's certainly true of travel writing. I'm not terribly interested in a destination or the name of a town or the name of the place that somebody wants to go to. What I *am* interested in is something that's new or different or changing or emerging. And that is always a result of what people are doing. So, for example, if Rwanda is opening up to tourism because the war is over and they're encouraging you to visit the gorillas in the mountains, that change has come about because people are doing things in a different way. In other words, a travel story is a live and moving thing. What we don't want is huge great tracts of 'here is a beautiful town in Italy and I'm going to describe it'.

AH: Does a travel story have to be shaped like articles in other parts of the newspaper?

CU: It can be but it doesn't have to be. My background is as a reporter so I've come from a consumer, newsy background. That's how Steve (Keenan) and Tom (Chesshyre) and, indeed, Chloë (Bryan-Brown) commission copy on our desk. I think all of us would say that travel journalism is a legitimate part of the general spectrum of journalism and, yes, sometimes you get to go to fabulous exotic places in the course of your research but the fundamental principles still apply. What is the story? What's the angle? What's new? What's going to work for our readers? It comes from thinking about what the readers are going to want to hear, not where do I want to go on my holidays or what sounds like an interesting destination for me as a travel writer? So if you're thinking about stories in the way that a news journalist would, I think then you are probably going to be coming up with suggestions that might suit our pages.

AH: Do you get a lot of material sent in from hopefuls?

cu: Yes, I get lots. I probably get about a hundred approaches a week, a lot of them on email and quite a few by post.

ah: Completed articles or ideas?

cu: Usually completed articles. That's the totally 'on spec' end of things. Then on top of that I probably get another fifty or sixty a week from journalists, maybe in another field, people wanting to be commissioned whom I don't necessarily know. They usually send ideas in. And then, of course, I get the regular writers whom I do know and have used before and they're constantly sending in ideas as well.

ah: Let's turn to the people you haven't published before, the hundred who send material in every week. What happens to these articles? Does somebody read them?

cu: Yes, usually I do or Steve or somebody on the desk, but I'm afraid to say that because we get so many would-be contributors, they don't get very long to impress me. You'd be amazed and probably horrified to see the way that some people pitch stuff to us. First of all, a lot of them don't bother to find out the name of the travel editor, yet my name or Steve's is in the paper almost every week. And so you get the feeling they're sending a general email around to lots and lots of different travel sections. Now my immediate response to that is to delete it, because I will not run the risk of accepting something that another paper might also accept. Also, if they are sending it to everybody they clearly have not read our section and thought about the sort of columns and slots and spaces we have and tailored it to our publication. For example, we have a slot called *Perfect Weekend* on the back page every Saturday. If you were thinking of doing a weekend break why not suggest why it fits that slot and that formula? If people don't bother to do that it suggests to me that they haven't taken the time and trouble to read the section, so why should I take the time and trouble to read their piece?

AH: Assuming writers have done their homework, how do you recognise quality? Let's start with an article submitted by somebody right outside the paper, outside travel writing, trying to break in.

CU: Well that was me, of course, about twelve years ago. I sent an on spec piece to the *Telegraph* where it was picked up by Bernice Davison and Sally Shalam who were working there at the time. I'd made an initial approach to Bernice suggesting some pieces based on my experiences backpacking for a year and she very kindly took the trouble to say, 'Well something on Mongolia would be great.' With that sliver of hope I wrote a piece which they accepted. So that shows that an on spec piece can get into the paper and lead to other things. But I think my advantage was that I was a trained journalist to start with and I'd been working as a reporter for quite a long time so I knew the tricks of the trade, if you like, to get something read. The intro is important, your whole premise that there's something new to say about a place is important and I imagine I must have got that across in the piece that I wrote for Bernice.

AH: Of the articles that come to you, how many have those qualities?

CU: Relatively few of the ones that come out of the blue. Some people have clearly thought it through and have put a stand-first, an introductory sentence at the top of their piece explaining what's new about it and why we should take it. That's great and I recommend it because we have relatively little time for close reading.

AH: About four or five lines?

CU: If that, just a sentence. More or less how it would appear on the page because we always have a headline and then a stand-first. What is *your* stand-first? Sell the story to me in twenty words, sum up why it's important. That's very helpful. It shows that you're thinking about how the story would work in a newspaper context. A lot of people make the mistake of assuming that their travels are so fascinating that I will be desperate to find a story hidden within the stuff that they send me. I can assure you that this is not the case. I always use the analogy of going to the pub with your holiday photos. If you're with a group of good friends the chances are they would like to see them because they know you. But a group of total strangers wouldn't be interested unless you were a photographer of world-class standard. It's the same with writing. It's no use writing about your holidays as though you were writing for your friends. What you need to do is to write for complete strangers whom you have to engage from the word go. Which is why you need a story, you need something new to tell, you need a snappy, well-crafted intro. All those things.

AH: Your predecessor at *The Times* used to say that a lot of what he had to go through was 'What I Did on My Hols'.

CU: Yes, we still get quite a lot of that which we simply can't publish because it's of very little interest to anyone other than the writer's immediate family and friends.

AH: But do you pick up a few new writers each year from those who are outside the travel-writing business?

CU: Yes. But they tend to be writers already of one sort or another. I can think of a couple of people we have started from scratch. Rob

Penn is one. He was a solicitor who gave that up to cycle round the world. When he came back full of stories he went on a photo-journalism training course. He's one of the few people who can write well and take very good photos too. He's now writing his first book, so that's great.

AH: It's clear that in your view, travel writing for newspapers is like any other journalism. You're really looking to avoid writers of deathless prose.

CU: We probably publish seven or eight hundred major features each year, so there's room for a huge variety of pieces. Start with the straightforward round-up-type pieces where someone's literally got on the phone to twenty companies and said, 'What's new in your programme of villa operators for France this season?' That's a simple information-gathering exercise. You've got to be thorough but it's not rocket science. It is the sort of thing that our readers like, though. So that is a very important element of what we're doing. At the other end of the scale you've got people who write absolutely beautiful prose that really conveys sense of place, or the destination, or the atmosphere, or the smell, or the mood. But you can't have everybody doing that and you can't have everybody doing round-ups. The key is to get the mix right.

AH: Could we take an overview of what you publish in a year? What do you do from season to season? I think people are often unaware of how cyclical travel writing is.

CU: Very broadly, and there are obviously exceptions to this, you are looking at skiing and winter sports coverage from about October to about April. In January and February, when people traditionally book their summer holidays (although increasingly they leave it till later) we do a lot of 'summer sun in the Med' pieces. By September people have come back from their summer holidays and are thinking about where to go in winter when it's cold here. That's when we do winter in the Caribbean or Indian Ocean or whatever. So you've got the general seasonal movements to consider as well as more specific slots. In early July, for example, we'll do an issue that's pretty much all about family holidays and how to prepare for your family holiday – whether it's financial planning, last-minute booking, dealing with problems or just last-minute ideas. And then there are features that are very much related to news stories. For example, this week we've done something on the row over changes to the US visa requirements. There are limited opportunities for freelance writers here because articles tend to be generated in-house quite late in the day. But looking at those issues might spark an idea for a broader piece.

AH: It's interesting that you divide up the world of travel writing into the hard-working items and the more reflective pieces about the world. And you're saying it's hard for outsiders to break in on the service side of journalism. But is that necessarily true? Suppose somebody got up something on travel insurance?

CU: Well if they can apply themselves to the subject and know a lot about it, there's no bar to that happening. But generally speaking those pieces are produced in-house or by regular contributors because these are the people who know the industry and we can rely on them to cover all the issues. I've no problem with people suggesting those types of pieces to me but I would need to be confident that they knew the industry, knew who the operators were and knew who to speak to.

AH: I take the point. Let us turn now to a different question but one that many people ask. Who pays for the journalist to travel?

CU: Obviously, people who submit stories on spec will have had to make their own arrangements. That is probably one reason why so many of these articles are write-ups of 'the holiday I happen to have had' rather than real travel stories in terms that a newspaper would appreciate. When a story *is* commissioned, *The Times* will sometimes pay, but in the normal run of things it doesn't have the budget; the cost is often borne by a national tourist board or a tour operator. But there is one tremendously important point here. Just because a tour operator pays, the journalist should not be in hock to that company, in fact, he or she *must not* be in hock to that company. It is like reviewing a product. Motoring writers don't pay for the car, but that quite rightly doesn't stop them criticising it. I don't expect writers to take any notice of who is paying the bills. There's one other, smaller point to bear in mind. Even if someone else is paying, you have to organise the trip yourself, which can be time-consuming. And you should worry about the cost in the sense that the trip you do should be appropriate to the piece you are writing. For example, don't go demanding five-star hotel suites if you are writing about a modest weekend break.

AH: You mention setting up a trip as time-consuming. Can we move now to the more detailed mechanics of getting a piece off the ground?

CU: Preparation is ninety per cent of writing a piece. I'll tell you what I do. I went to Sri Lanka in November and did a piece that appeared a couple of weeks ago. My preparation included reading what other people had written about Sri Lanka, whether it was newspaper articles or guidebooks, all of which I read closely before I went. This gave me some ideas about things I would love to see and do when I was there. I looked at some websites and I looked through the brochures put out by tour operators to get an idea of what was on offer. I also read some slightly more specialist books including one about the work of the architect Geoffrey Bawa. I wrote a little piece about him to go with my main feature. And I talked to people who'd been to Sri Lanka and who knew it well.

AH: Did you make appointments to meet people in Sri Lanka?

CU: Absolutely. I planned an itinerary. That's not always ideal. Sometimes you just want to go off the itinerary because something's caught your fancy but I had a pretty clear idea of who I was going to be meeting and roughly when and what we were going to be talking about. Some of it was left to the last minute to sort out but it all worked out brilliantly.

AH: How long did you spend on preparation?

CU: About two months.

AH: So you are probably preparing a lot of pieces simultaneously?

CU: Yes, I am constantly setting stuff up. I'm wanting to go to Athens in February and I'm working on that now. But I'm also planning a trip to the Crimea in April and May. I've just read a book on the history of the Ukraine. I always have books on the go that are relevant to the places I'm going to.

AH: It's clear that travel writing is not just a matter of having a wonderful experience.

CU: No, although it can be. For example, I did an overland trip with Dragoman where I was on a truck with ten other people for two weeks. That was a story in itself. But in Sri Lanka, a lot of what I did was visiting hotels which can be quite boring, but you do need to know about them. There was a lot in my story about what new hotels there are. I also saw some of the key sites. For example, I climbed the rock temple at Sigiriya. Then again, I spent one or two mornings mooching about in a market and on the beach just to get a flavour of the atmosphere; do people get hassled, are drinks expensive, what's the food like? So sometimes I'm doing something quite structured like visiting a hotel and talking to the general manager, and sometimes I'm spending half a day just wandering about a town. But what I am not doing, unfortunately, is lying on a beach.

AH: That was one of the great shocks for me when I began travel writing. You see other people's swimming pools; you don't get to swim in them.

CU: Exactly. I spent a little time on Unawatuna Beach which is very popular but after fifteen minutes I knew all I needed to know about it and sunbathing there for three hours wouldn't have given me much more copy.

AH: So the advice is to keep your mind on research, even when you are accumulating descriptive material?

CU: Certainly there are pieces where spending a lovely, lazy day on a boat or a beach is important and is part of the copy. If you're rushing from place to place too much you do miss out on atmosphere. One of the great things about the Caribbean, for example, is having a leisurely breakfast on your balcony with little birds flitting around, taking in a lovely view and not worrying about fast service or any of those things the Caribbean doesn't really do very well. There's no compulsion to be constantly chasing your tail all the time.

AH: I guess within a piece on the Caribbean, having breakfast on your balcony is a little anecdote. Now if a piece has quite a few anecdotes, are most of them about people?

CU: They probably would be, yes. Because that's what's going to be of greatest interest – what people are saying or doing that's witty or apposite or interesting. It's very hard to be consistently interesting if you're writing just about yourself or your reaction to things. It's helpful to get the reactions of other holidaymakers. You might take against a place greatly – I often do – but if the people who're actually paying to stay in the hotel like it, then it's worth recording that.

AH: So all this time you're filling up a thick notebook?

CU: Absolutely. I come back from every trip with a notebook full of impressions and quotes and comments.

AH: And then the process of writing. Do you read your notebook before you write? Or do you look up your notebook when you're in doubt?

CU: Yes, I'm boringly thorough about this. I go through my notes and generally I type them up. Not all of them. But I type selectively the most interesting bits. And the process of doing this means it really goes into my head. I know if I've done my research properly because writing the piece is easy. Occasionally if I struggle it's because I haven't done enough research.

A View from the Armchair

Travel writer Adam Hopkins selects the best of travellers'
tales and reveals the secret of their success

It may be daunting to survey the scene and ask yourself, 'Where do I fit in?' The shelves of Britain's libraries, or more to the point in this case Britain's bookshops, sag with the weight of travel books: proper travel books as well as guides. There are far more than you will find in their French or Spanish or Italian equivalents. They range from undisputed works of literature to read-it-on-the-beach-and-then-chuck-it paperbacks – something for everybody and something, you may think, for every writer. For while it is very nice to go travelling, it's also oh so nice to write about it.

But before the plunge into the types and tactics of travel books, and a look at some works, great and small, good and bad, that all of us might study with advantage, it is probably just as well to clear the ground by asking ourselves why there should be so much excellent British travel writing. It is a tradition into which each one of us, writer or would-be writer of travel, may be able to tap usefully.

One standard view is that the British are an island race and have to travel properly to get anywhere at all: once they were imperialists, now they are post-imperialists. What do you expect when they travel so much – and often travel so seriously, full of exploratory intent? Plausible, to a degree, I think, but only going part of the way. For the fact is that travel writing as we know it could never have developed without a comparable richness in another form of writing in which Britain also specialises: biography and especially autobiography. Of this, our islands have produced far more than other European countries. Americans, who are no slouches at travel writing, are also strong on writing about real people; and they are important to us, quite apart from the merits of their books, since they compete directly with British writers.

The fact of the matter is that travel writing is the art of bringing together travel and autobiography (and in some cases, its smaller cousin, the diary). That mixture is its starting point. Its practitioners need an intense interest in the world around them and also, rather embarrassingly, quite a fair interest in themselves. Some writers deal especially in emotions, they try to evoke their own experiences of 'abroad' with nostalgia or delight and often humour; others go adventuring and live (one hopes) to tell rip-roaring yarns about themselves and their companions, quite often full of personal insights; while others again, and some of the finest, try to be clear mirrors to the world – they aim to tell their readers something interesting or useful about a place. But always, however it is handled, even if it is concealed, the writer's self is present. It cannot be otherwise. The writing is the voice of an individual in his or her relationship with a special kind of experience. That is one of the identifying marks of travel writing. First, find your voice.

Yet 'travel' in the sense of 'travel books' does not have to mean simply going to places; it can also mean *being* in places, an evocation of a town, an island, a special countryside – books in which, as the writer Lawrence Durrell once remarked, nothing very much happens. And none the worse for that. These are the books of emotion and atmosphere, what one might call the Shangri-La persuasion.

Shangri-La

Let's begin, then, at a practical level with a trend or genre which is particularly popular today.

Over the past decade or two and right up into the present, an extraordinary number of the many 'travel' books about 'abroad' in a fixed setting have been concerned with buying and doing up houses. Inevitably my choice here will be personal, if not downright quirky, for the simple reason that there are so many to choose from. But here are four to open the wider debate on travel writing, all of them 'Shangri-La' housing tales: Frances Mayes' *Under the Tuscan Sun*; Emma Tennant's *A House in Corfu*; the late Derek Lambert's *Spanish Lessons*; and Peter Mayle's famous – or notorious – slim volume, *A Year in Provence*. None could be described as classics; all are open to quite serious criticism, yet all employ formulae that have made them popular. (Personally, though, to show my cards before the argument begins, I think that Peter Mayle has been most unfairly criticised and I like *Provence* very much.)

Frances Mayes', then, to take a first book at random, belongs to a school of travel writing in which, so far as possible, everything is bejewelled. Here she is on eating grapes.

'...I see a man in a sweater, despite the heat. The trunk of his minuscule Fiat is piled with black grapes that have warmed all morning in the sun. I'm stopped by the winy, musty, violet [sic] scents. He offers me one. The hot sweetness breaks open in my mouth. I have never tasted anything so essential in my life as this grape on this morning. They even smell purple [hang on, they were black a moment back or possibly violet]. The flavor [for we have started with an American writer], older than the Etruscans and deeply fresh and pleasing, just leaves me stunned.'

It's highly wrought throughout, if sometimes a bit off-beam, 'poetical' you might say if you wished to be hostile. It makes a claim to special insider knowledge: she and her partner are always off to restaurants which their 'many guidebooks never mentioned'. That is to say, like many, many travel books it is firmly anti-tourist and possibly its implicit snobbism is pleasing to readers. All of us, alas, like being on the inside circuit, being in the know. But for all that – and gaining plus points for her intense interest in food, another major selling point in many, many modern travel books – Mayes builds up little by little an attractive picture of an old house and its coming together to offer a new life in a place with which the writer has passionately identified. Perhaps the passion is the point and so too is the identification, for Frances Mayes has stirred many a soul to the point of imitation.

Long ago Evelyn Waugh put the boot into this type of writing with a long, lyrical, painterly description of a sunset over Mount Etna. It ended, suddenly and totally unexpectedly, with the words 'Nothing I have ever seen in Art or Nature was quite so revolting.' Like it or not, however, Mayes' kind of Shangri-La writing endures and is one of the options for writers of her kind of sensibility. Readers can't seem to get enough of it.

Emma Tennant's *A House in Corfu* is far more modest in the sense that gasps and unlikely metaphors are strewn about less thickly. At a personal level she is also rather reticent. The book is about her parents building a house in what, back in the 1960s, was a remote bay (tourism was soon to follow them, right into their own bay and, though troubled in practical terms, she shows no sign of believing it was iniquitous for it to come there), but she tells us little about herself or her relationships, although they figure obliquely. There is just a little more about her parents, so that they live as characters within the enterprise. In other words it is perhaps a trifle thin in the personal sense. But little by little she too builds up a satisfying and convincing picture, not so much of the house, as of Corfu as it was at a particular moment in time. You feel her villagers are real villagers and the workmen are real individual workmen. Her flowers in the olive groves are right there, lovely but comparatively unhyped. Myself, I found the book rather sad, especially the death of the author's father, but it's no surprise that the quote from the *Daily Telegraph* displayed on the front cover, and therefore editorially endorsed, describes it as 'a study in happiness and how to achieve it'.

Deep down the pursuit of happiness is the real object of the Shangri-La writer. There's nothing wrong with that at all – it's often highly popular – but there are many problems of tone to solve. Will you go for it gaudily, and with or without an element of restraint on the personal front?

As to the other 'house' books on my table, Derek Lambert's *Spanish Lessons* (chosen here since it came out later than Chris Stewart's excellent *Driving Over Lemons*, also set in Spain) tells the story of a British journalist and his wife struggling, like Frances Mayes, to do up an old house. Here few claims are made to the house's beauty, nor would you necessarily expect them in a good hardworking volume by a journalist. It does convey plenty of atmosphere – there is a good passage on a local shop, for instance, which, like some of the best poems of Walt Whitman, is simply a list, in this case of all the extraordinary objects that can be bought there. *Spanish Lessons*, at quite a deep level, is a book about struggling to hang on to the house against the vagaries and financial pressures of a freelance writer's life (would-be writers, be warned by Derek Lambert: money is never easy when you live by the pen). But in all this it is also very, very funny.

The humour is achieved by a quite different tactic from anything employed by Mayes or Tennant, though it is very common in travel writing: the shaping of reality to form a series of succinct short

stories, one to a chapter with a few bits about the area bolted on.
It's an excellent device so long as the reader is lulled into mistaking
the tales for true and does not immediately rumble their artful
construction (you can use it in one book, but maybe not in two,
witness Chris Stewart's much less successful, second volume *A
Parrot in the Pepper Tree*). But this construction has an even greater
disadvantage to my mind. In looking for comic twists, the writer is
often obliged to make his characters into pub storytellers' 'types'.
People like reading this but in the end, the more it's done, the more
you hear about 'types', the less you learn about the country, the less
the documentary value of the book.

The great question about Peter Mayle's *A Year in Provence* is
whether his book, greeted rapturously on publication and with
more than a touch of jealous criticism as its staggering success
became apparent, has gone too far down this line. Some say that in
presenting his neighbours as comic characters, he has sold them
down the river with Anglo-Saxon insouciance. I confess I liked it on
first reading and indeed on reading it again with this question in
my mind. For even if Mayle's builders never come on time, in a
manner put forward as especially Provençal (a little bit of stereotyp-
ing here or is it true?), their work when they do arrive is heroic and
determined, not to say artistic. And the workmen and farmers and
restaurateurs are so various and peculiar you cannot believe they
are entirely made up. There's the plumber who plays the clarinet to
keep his fingers nimble when it's too cold to work, for instance, and
the beer-drinking plasterer who does it all with trowel, hand and
wrist and the moment it's finished it looks old and human. I am
persuaded that Peter Mayle not only relishes his characters but
loves them (just as he does his food; there are some succulent
passages on eating out).

As to the other common charge that he's destroyed Provence by
writing about it in a way that attracts the tourists, a recent BBC

radio programme decided that apart from sightseers coming directly to his house, the changes that were happening were happening everywhere: more cars, more mobile phones and, yes, more tourists. It's the way of the world: don't always blame the travel writer. He gets there first but his arrival is a sign that others are not far behind. Nor is it always graceful for a writer to despise tourists when their presence is so devoutly desired by those who live in crumbling rural economies.

At all events, writing about houses is a major genre, providing an insight into people (including the author of the book) in a particular place, generally within a broad atmosphere of happiness. You can write it as pseudo-poetry, or close observation or short stories, as a mixture, or as something else entirely new and different, which is, of course, always the best if you are lucky enough to be one of the few originals. All of this applies to all travel writing.

As to place, Provence is possibly worked out, at least for the moment, but how about the Lot valley? Tuscany seems an ever-rich vein, but why not Puglia as well? And as for Spain, the going is still good, with Portugal no doubt to follow. All these are places which are near, relatively easy to reach and easily imaginable by readers. Myself, having become aware of people now buying homes in Sri Lanka, I cannot believe the first volume is far away, and with it, possibly, a new approach. But do be warned, the publishers may not agree. What counts is what you can get published.

There is another way, however, of pursuing happiness, which often yields a much more profound and satisfying travel book. That is by way of time elapsed. Gerald Durrell, in *My Family and other Animals*, evoked his Corfu childhood with huge charm and skill, and, of course, humour. He too has been accused of writing in 'types' but here – to intrude a personal note – I have to disagree. Quite some years after his book appeared, I got to know one of his greatest characters, the marvellous child-delighting naturalist Dr

Theodore Stephanides. He was just as Gerald Durrell had described him – long-bearded and compassionate, a source of endless entertainment and expansion of the mind, a deeply memorable man. Durrell was dealing in reality about Corfu; however tall some of his stories, there was a bedrock there. But over it all, as he told the story, there lay a gentle blue rinse of nostalgia. That is the point. In looking backwards we see different patterns. Here he has done it in a way that many find compulsive; one hopes that, light as it is, this is a book that will endure.

This thought, almost inevitably, ushers in two other writers. Laurie Lee spent all his life looking back over what was really a short, though intense, span of his life: childhood and his time as a young man, in Gloucester and Spain. The result was a trilogy: *Cider with Rosie*, an autobiography of his early years, the delightful *As I Walked Out One Midsummer Morning*, and his last and very moving *A Moment of War*, which raised doubts among many readers as to its veracity over the Spanish Civil War. *As I Walked Out* tells how he busked across Spain in the 1930s. Deeply nostalgic, it is the perfect travel book on a small scale, an observant autobiography, full of a young man's lyricism, full of people and self, and at the same time surprisingly direct and tough about such matters as sex and violence. It is the fruit of long and deep emotional, not necessarily intellectual, reflection.

And then there is a greater master, still writing, if not so very often, and always, increasingly, revered both among readers and the many travel writers who salute him in their texts: Patrick Leigh Fermor.

Leigh Fermor began his adult life, while many of his contemporaries were still in school, by walking from Holland to Constantinople. During World War II his capture of the German General Kreipe and his flight with his captive through the mountains of Crete (described in Stanley Moss's *Ill Met by Moonlight*) was one of the greatest acts of derring-do of the mid-twentieth century. He went on to write his own books, of course. *Mani* and *Roumeli* are both travel books about 'old' Greece, with a slender narrative thread and plenty of historical learning and imagination. These were aspects of his writing he was to develop further. For since the 1970s, Leigh Fermor has been slowly publishing an account of his youthful passage across Europe (with one volume in the trilogy still to come).

A Time of Gifts and *Between the Woods and the Water* are simply among the best books of the past twenty-five or thirty years, whether in 'travel' or other genres, and every apprentice travel writer should study them: not that we can, or should, hope to imitate him. Really it is a matter of a deeply and often poetic observation set out in a language rich with surprising metaphors which turn out to be so just, so appropriate, they stop the reader in his tracks. But equally, the joy lies in the constant play on historical continuities, always learned and often surprising, which he uses to illuminate landscapes and peoples. His books are treasure chests, to be opened every now and then, their contents looked at carefully, then packed away again for another day.

Gone on an adventure

Patrick Leigh Fermor's young man's journey was an adventure, though he never harps on it, a very great adventure. And adventuring, far more than doing up old houses, has produced some of the greatest and most enduring travel writing. Since almost by definition we cannot hope to make the journey for ourselves, the reader is required to do no more than identify with the writer and feel the pains and thrills and the emotion without ever stirring far from the fireside. No wonder it sells so well. And since so much of adventuring takes place in remote parts and is so often concerned with older lifestyles – not to say the Noble Savage – it often tells us much, with evident regret, of a world that is disappearing. (With the passage of time, much travel writing starts to read like snapshots of a distant past. This is an incidental benefit for the reader quite unintended by the writer.)

One point worth noting right at the beginning, is that some of the greatest exemplars of hard travelling and adventure writing have been women.

Freya Stark is one, and though she was born in 1893, her influence on travel writing is still felt, again very often in a poetical-reflective style which yields a startling sense of revelation. Her patch was Arabia Magna, with excursions into Greece and furthest Asia. In the words of the critic Margaret Lane, her 'spirit was drawn to deserts and burning suns'. She was a traveller of the greatest hardiness and boldness, ready if need be to contemplate her own death. And the books came tumbling out, with names still familiar to many – *The Valleys of the Assassins* (1934), *The Lycian Shore* of 1956, and so on. One of the points her would-be followers (never say imitators) may care to note is that she was wonderfully well prepared. Highly educated, her young days spent taking in the classics in a substantial way, she learned Arabic at the (London) School of Oriental Studies. She married late and travelled alone – so far as she could. It was necessarily not quite alone, in a world of bearers and helpers. The reader admires her as a woman finding herself in difficult places, is moved by her descriptions and must at least consider her analysis. There is much here that is entirely admirable and may well serve as an inspiration to men and women alike.

But Freya Stark too illustrates a difficulty I have already touched upon (in the more limited terms of the travel writer's general dislike of tourists and modern ways). At a deeper level, it is this: how can the writer respond without condescension to the wishes of poor people to escape a lot which they themselves quite plainly see as more primitive than it has to be?

Here she is on that familiar theme, the way that 'progress' spoils it all. She hopes to leave the charm and independence of Arabia intact, she says, continuing:

'I think there is no way to do this and to keep alive the Arab's happiness in his own virtues except to live his life in certain measure. One may differ in material ways; one may sit on chairs and use forks and gramophones; but on no account must one put before people, so easily beguiled, a set of values different from their own. Discontent with their standards is the first step in the degradation of the East.'

So there you have it. Freya Stark is wonderful and in most respects a model for aspirants both male and female but this kind of question needs to be handled today with much greater sensitivity. At the same time, one can scarcely deny the relevance of the thought. Think of alcoholism among the Inuit. Think of the effect of Western-style diseases on the Amazon peoples. Think of the plight of the indigenous peoples of Australia. Think, also, of the Marsh Arabs of Iraq. Today, when you come to a work like *The Marsh Arabs* (of Iraq) by another fine travel writer of the same school, Wilfred Thesiger, it reads with hindsight like a lament for a people who have been lost, tragically reduced by the ministrations of the modern world. It should also be said that at the time when Thesiger stayed among them, before the persecution by Saddam Hussein, they were often dying of grotesque diseases which his curious amateur doctoring could not alleviate.

Perhaps the dark view of the future is often right. What I am saying is that the modern travel writer should not despise automatically comforts and pleasures such as DVDs and fast roads, that he himself takes entirely for granted. The world is changing. You have to get used to that.

Speaking of women writers, though, the Irish author Dervla Murphy is another intrepid woman traveller. She has been at it quite a while now, alone or with her daughter. Compared to Freya Stark her preparation is negligible. She seems to have no foreign languages to speak of; her historical knowledge is shallow, though she has some very handy introductions to useful people along the way. But goodness she gives it all a go, and one reads on, and on, drawn by her spunkiness, her unwillingness to give up, her amazing *sang-froid*. Here she shoots a wolf attacking her by night (though some friends, she cheerfully allows, thought it might have been just wild dogs). Here she goes riding (and pushing) her beloved bike Roz over almost trackless mountain and desert. (Roz is undoubtedly her best friend; Murphy usually uses 'we' to mean herself and bike, the name being short for Rosinante, which is, of course, also Don Quixote's horse.) In due course she pushes Roz clear over the Shibar Pass in the Hindu Kush in deep Afghanistan, on her way from England to India, with admiration for the mountain views and total lack of any (declared) sense that she is doing anything unusual. A little later in the same book, when she comes to the Khyber Pass, she finds it an anti-climax after the Shibar, her reactions described in as matter-of-fact a way as if she was comparing Cox's Pippins to Golden Delicious.

Personally, more out of prejudice, perhaps, than resistance to a form that is often popular, I'm dead against gimmicks as a way to launch a story – 'My Travels on a Broken Skateboard', 'My Travels with a Wild Bull on the Back Seat of a Seat 600'. The trouble is they often sell well for a short while. As regards Roz, you might think Dervla Murphy's cycling addiction was a gimmick. But the more you read the more convinced you are. She is cycling because she likes it, it is all an adventure. The pleasure it gives to readers is a measure of her absolutely adventurous, absolutely one-off nature.

In that early cycling book of hers, *Full Tilt*, she introduces the

Hindu Kush. This wonderful range has been a magnet to travellers and travel writers during the past century, no doubt with more to come if you can dodge the bullets. She herself loved it so much she was tempted to think of settling there. Eric Newby walked off into it quite a few years earlier bound on an adventure of his own, recounted in *A Short Walk in the Hindu Kush*. It was quite a risky one, from which he was lucky to come back in one piece. On his return he encountered Wilfred Thesiger on one of his own grand progresses of exploration. Newby is nothing if not funny – often, especially in this book, he makes you laugh aloud. He and his travelling-companion Hugh were only too aware as they parleyed with Thesiger at his camp of the poor impression their own rank amateurishness was creating on the (already) great man.

Thesiger talks to them, with relish, of the surgery he has performed among the Arabs, cutting off fingers, taking out an eye. Eventually, they prepare to turn in for the night. 'The ground was like iron with sharp rocks sticking up out of it. We started to blow up our air-beds. "God, you must be a couple of pansies," said Thesiger.' And so the book concludes.

Newby proves, as Thesiger markedly does not, that comedy and adventure can go together. *A Short Walk in the Hindu Kush* is prescribed reading for anyone who ever hopes to strike a lighter note, relying as it does on self-deprecation (in the old English style) and flashes of quick, unexpected wit.

The same is true, for me, of another adventurous writer, very much of our own times – Redmond O'Hanlon. His books, whether set in Borneo or up the Amazon, are ventures into the absurd. You can't imagine how such a duffer gets by. But a word of warning here, for O'Hanlon is not at all what he seems in his own self-presentation within the books. He is a learned, literary man, a self-conscious artist, and everything he writes is written for a carefully thought-out purpose. Thank heavens, then, that a large part of his purpose is humour. And one might say the same of a less-known but equally funny writer, Nigel Barley, a professional anthropologist whose work takes him into ever more comical and curious corners, though without a hint of condescension. Both Barley and O'Hanlon are worthy of study.

Humorous or not so humorous, however, there is another kind of travelling adventure that should at least be logged. This is the Quest. Whether the Quest is real or clearly just a peg to hang a book on (the worst kind of Quest, in my view), it can be a very good way of organising both a journey and the way a writer writes about it. The basic tactic is extremely obvious, but provides a narrative thread, around which all the travel writer's skills may be deployed. There are many books in this class but let me mention just one: *Chasing the Monsoon*, by Alexander Frater, in which the author follows the progress of the monsoon from the Indian south to north, engaging in wonderful discussions and pleasurable studies of Indian thought processes. There are fine anecdotes as well. This is another admirable book, which should certainly be on the tyro's booklist.

The clear mirror: looking at the world out there

Every one of the writers already mentioned tells you about the countries he or she has visited, some a little, others a great deal. But the places themselves are seen as part of an autobiographical arrangement. Self is openly a major subject, a large part of the performance. The writing of these books can be very comfortable, an easement to the ego, but if, and only if, you have a sympathetic and interesting persona to offer. Which brings us round again to that essential, the need for every writer to find his or her own voice.

Bearing that *sine qua non* in mind, there is another school of travel writing in which, though the self is often visible, the focus is much more resolutely on the world out there. These are travel books of real, non-egotistical inquiry.

Since India has always been one of the beloved subjects among British travel writers, and their readers, let's start with another book on the subcontinent.

William Dalrymple is still a relatively young man. He has already turned in several quite outstanding travel books (including *In Xanadu*, written when he was twenty-two) and at least one enthralling work of history, *White Mughals*. The book which is perhaps most interesting in this discussion is his portrait of Delhi, *City of Djinns*. It is something of a crossover in style, containing a distinct element of the short story alongside a running narrative based on his own life in Delhi, often observed with great humour. But it is not himself he is concentrating on at all, rather it is what he sees and hears. He is a very intelligent writer, though not in the least wearisomely so. Woven through his narrative is perhaps the strongest historical awareness of any writer named so far, except Leigh Fermor, as he contemplates the city:

> 'Though it has been burned by invaders time and time again, millennium after millennium, still the city was rebuilt; each time it rose like a phoenix from the fire. Just as the Hindus believe that a body will be reincarnated over and over again until it becomes perfect, so it seemed Delhi was destined to appear over and over again in a new incarnation century after century.'

The history is deployed in a series of flashbacks running backwards in time from the assassination of Mrs Gandhi and the anti-Sikh riots which followed, all the way to the *Mahabharata* and almost the start of time. The stories are often told by contemporary Indians, historians and archaeologists, in conversation, on the spot. Dalrymple offers them as thinking bridges between past and present.

It is excellent stuff and with Dalrymple in mind, I can scarcely stress enough the importance of a sense of history for the travel writer who hopes to offer understanding as well as mere depiction.

Jan Morris also has a great sense of history, often deployed on Indian subjects. But just to venture back to Europe for a moment and to her (relatively early) book, *Spain*, written in a huge hurry to meet a contract. This is now somewhat out of date, but still a touchstone if you want to understand Spain, or at least the Spain from which post-1975 democracy has flowed.

In terms of the writer's personality you have but to pick up the book to recognise the style as Jan Morris. 'In the Condestable chapel, beyond the high altar, there lies upon his splendid tomb Don Pedro Hernandez de Velasco, Hereditary Constable of Castile, who died in the fifteenth century but whose marble thick-veined hands still warily grasp his sword-hilt,' writes Morris, to take a single sentence, entirely at random.

Here is all the customary sonority, the sense of style, the unmistakably Morrisian phrase 'marble thick-veined hands'. You know at once whom you are reading, but though the author was in fact belting around Spain in a camper van, the personal narrative never appears at all. Indeed the personal pronoun 'I' is just occasionally deployed to express an opinion, as in 'I think . . .' Otherwise it hardly appears all. All rests on the observation, the analysis and in Jan Morris's case, sometimes to a fault, the flow and energy of language. The self is obscured but visible at the same time, a characteristic of many of the finest writers.

Norman Lewis is another in the great school of observation, though in practice his journeys were often rather brief. His prose is much lighter and more modest, say, than Morris's, but often extremely memorable. His books are friends, though he too portrays a world that is often under threat. He presents a village in coastal Catalonia, for instance, in *Voices of the Old Sea*, changed irrevocably by a season's tourism. But here the treatment is more subtle. There is melancholy, yes, but also an acknowledgement that all is not over yet, that optimism is a possible response.

Lewis is a man who isn't involved in any argument about himself or his identity. The 'I' is a lever for anecdote, a guarantee that his are the observing eyes, a part of his classic act, balanced and humane, bringing us good reason for indignation or pleasure, laughter or simply astonishment. More than almost anyone else his subject is the world out there.

The only obvious rival in this is Colin Thubron, who sets off, often in rather a deliberate style, to cover his chosen territory, whether it is China, Russia or Siberia. But he quickly leaps over the hurdle of his own deliberation. *In Siberia* is the most recent of his large-scale travels and here he often achieves in his portrayal, both of people and of travelling in this enormous landscape, a pure poetry based on observation and exactitude. Siberia is struggling with its post-Soviet collapse, with fearful difficulties yet here too marvels are achieved, the human spirit glows.

'A traveller needs to believe in the significance of where he is, and therefore in his own meaning,' says Thubron. But his self is a sounding board, never an obtrusion. More than almost any of his contemporaries, except perhaps V. S. Naipaul (see *India, a Million Mutinies Now*), he proceeds by conversations, often long ones. He is also, again, a most modest, true adventurer. There is a chapter with magnificent descriptions and extraordinary, out-of-this world conversations, in which he takes a river boat deep into the Arctic and disembarks at a village so shockingly run down that even the crew of the river steamer beg him not to go ashore. He does; and the only bed he can find is in the hospital, where he shares his part of the premises with an old man of one of the indigenous tribes.

'An elastic band which he bound around his head prevented it, he said, from flying apart. Sometimes he sat in the vestibule as if waiting for someone who did not come.'

And so the passage about the patient ends. This is the plain and simple language, and faithful reporting – not on this occasion without pathos – of a true traveller and of a truth-telling writer. You could not deny that his is a high calling. To follow in his footsteps, you require thorough advance study, bravery and a great capacity to persist. And all that before you write a word.

Other voices, other directions

Paul Theroux, Jonathan Raban, Bill Bryson with his jokes – we live at a time of marvellous travel writing and to add to the best is a fine aspiration. At a more practical level, you might just possibly make a little money, though not much, unless you are very, very lucky and hit the right time with the right book. It is, perhaps, more a lifestyle than a living.

But the subjects and the directions travel writing can take are endless, for what is reflected in books of travel is human life. Elizabeth Romer's *The Tuscan Year* was one of the earlier books to run recipes alongside narrative, month-by-month in this case, often a useful device. Gijs van Hensbergen's delightful *In the Kitchens of Castile*, an account of working in a restaurant in Segovia, might well be claimed as a travel book. I am a little doubtful about Literary Companions, such as the series published by John Murray, but under the adventure heading I would certainly like to claim Joe Simpson's moral tale of mountaineering, *Touching the Void*, a truly remarkable book. Some novels have more than a touch of travel writing.

So there are plenty of ways for the new writer to go. What's needed is a fair whack of reading, a litre or two of thoughtful, sensitive, intelligent and possibly daring travel, a never-flagging interest in people, an interesting and perhaps unusual way of writing about it all and then you are in business. Although let's not forget one small detail – a supportive publisher. Easy? Not really. But the game is beautiful.

Adam Hopkins is an author, journalist and academic. His travel books include: Crete: its Past, Present and People; Holland: Its History, Paintings and People; *and* Spanish Journeys, a Portrait of Spain. *He has contributed on travel to a wide variety of publications, in recent years particularly to the* Daily Telegraph, The Times *and the* Financial Times. *He lives much of the year in remote western Spain. In winter, he teaches at the University of Westminster in London.*

From Here to There and Back Again

Ruth Jarvis, series editor for Time Out Guides,
*and Mark Ellingham, series editor for and founder
of* Rough Guides, *talk to Daniel Smith about what
it takes to be a guide writer*

DANIEL SMITH: What are you looking for when you're commissioning writers?

MARK ELLINGHAM: It depends whether it's a new book or a revised edition. Ninety per cent of what we do is revised editions and we will always go back to the original authors. Our authors earn royalties on their books. Most of the other guides pay fees but in many ways we think that having royaltied authors produces a greater commitment to devoting the best part of a year of your life to writing a book.

If we're looking for a completely new author, we want somebody who is fascinated by all aspects of their destination. A guidebook writer has to be an extraordinary polymath, communicating an enthusiasm and knowledge. If you're writing on Spain, you have to know about everything from Romanesque architecture to football, from local wine to adventure sports.

RUTH JARVIS: Every guidebook company puts its titles together slightly differently and we use a team of local writers. We look for people with knowledge of a specialist field: the film writer needs to be a cinema obsessive, the restaurant writers to eat out frequently; often they already write on the subject for local publications. For the sightseeing sections we like to use writers who either know the part of town they're writing about really well – merely living there isn't always enough – or are fascinated by it and keen to research. And for background chapters and boxes we like to throw a few specialists into the mix: people who have a particular perspective or a preoccupation.

ME: At *Rough Guides* we have some locally based authors but the majority are not. However, our writers tend to have a travel background and go to the area they're covering very regularly. You can argue it all sorts of ways. Perhaps you get a fresher perspective if you're not actually living in the place but on the other hand the insider's view may be better informed.

DS: Is it important for your writers to have a track record in travel writing?

ME: No, not necessarily. We quite often take people straight out of university to work on updates or even new books. And we use people who are taking a career break in their thirties or forties and the odd retired person as well. The guy who updated our Morocco book for many years was retired. Lots of people like to travel after they retire; it provides them with a focus and an income.

But I would say pretty much everybody who comes to us has done some sort of writing previously, even if it's just on a student paper. There is a huge amount of words that go into a guide and it really is quite a feat of sustained writing. So some experience is important. But there's a whole mix of people with different reasons for wanting to do travel writing, all with different ways of operating.

RJ: Our writers have varied backgrounds. It helps a lot if they've worked on a local listings magazine or an English-language publication, depending on whereabouts in the world we're dealing with. You do get some guidebook professionals but the odds are that many we use will be critics for magazines. A lot of guidebook writers will also turn in the odd feature for Condé Nast or websites across the world. But I never totally trust people's CVs. And I do enough copy editing myself to know how a good copy editor can flatter a poor writer's skills.

It doesn't really matter if they're not great travellers. Our consultant editor and primary writer on the Las Vegas guide, James Reza, is afraid of flying and he lives in Vegas which is a desert drive away from pretty much anywhere. He's never been out of the country but he keeps up.

DS: So how do you go about choosing your writers?

RJ: Like everyone else in the industry, I am looking for writers who can follow a brief and hand in readable copy on time. I pick up on signs of professionalism. It makes no difference whether I've approached them or they've approached me. I look for the same qualities. That's to say I look for concise emails and for speed in replying. If somebody can't get back to me on email for four days, then they're going to be late with their copy. And I look for a good writing style in emails as well. Then I arrange to meet that person in a bar or a coffee shop or restaurant in the city we're covering. I'll go away with their cuttings and I will typically ask them to write a review of the place where we've just met in the style of a *Time Out* guide. They have to be reasonably detached and realistic. We don't do tourism PR and a lot of people find that is their natural style.

ME: We sometimes advertise for authors when we're running a bit short and we'll give them a test. We may ask them to send us a brief rough guide to somewhere they know well. We have an awful lot of people writing in and we prefer it if they say exactly what they want to do. If somebody just says they really want to work on our guides, it doesn't help us to place them. We are more interested if it's somebody saying that they speak very good Latin American Spanish and spent six months in Peru and want to work on the next edition of that book and here's how it could be improved.

DS: So you want writers who bring some kind of angle to what they write?

RJ: We don't like what we call 'guidebook bollocks' but we don't like neutral content either. We do want to be reasonably opinionated. But they shouldn't have to try too hard for it. There are various types of writers who you come across again and again. There is always one guy – and it normally is a guy – who writes really pithy, fantastic reviews of bars, restaurants, music venues. They're droll and wry and they know what they're talking about. They're vaguely obsessive. It's good to have obsessives on guides as long as they can also surface into the real world and remember that visitors also occasionally need a little bit of entry-level information. In a way, we want to make some initial choices for our readers that are not necessarily based on what's most popular or most touristy.

ME: Absolutely we want writers with strong personalities. There is a genre of guidebook writing which is lacking any sort of personality. You find it with many of the highly illustrated guides. Our guidebooks have always been highly opinionated and I think people like them for that.

DS: Is the guidebook market overcrowded?

RJ: No, amazingly. Travel abroad from this country is three times as popular as it was twenty years ago and so guides are part of an expanding book market. With the insecurity around travel at the moment, particularly in the USA, I am sure some of our competitors have had to tighten their belts but we haven't. In fact, we've put on readership since September 11, both in the States and here.

We try to differentiate ourselves from the competition by developing our own tone, using local writers and having lots of full-colour photos. But I think the public's opinion of titles depends mostly on their personal experience of them. There might be a particularly bad guide in any series which sends people to a venue which closed two years ago and then they'll never use that series again. If they have a good time on a trip using a particular guidebook, however, then they will probably go back to that series.

ME: I think the market is overcrowded. We like to think we produce well-written books and have perhaps a more serious treatment of culture than some of the competition. In the past some of the reviews of *Lonely Planet* have said they are books written by travellers who end up writing and ours are written by writers who end up travelling. You can't be too exact in that but we do pride ourselves in taking a great deal of care and we edit very heavily.

If you're conceiving a new travel guide now, it's not impossible but it either has to be very brilliant or have an extraordinary new concept to break through in the mainstream. There's always space for individual niche guides and I think there's always space for local guides which are a bit off the road for the larger publishers. When you have a national sales force you have to do a bit more than 3,000 sales each year, but a local publisher can get away with that and make a profit.

RJ: Absolutely. For example, we were looking at a guide to Reykjavik but we didn't do it in the end because we figured out we would need about one in every eight English-speaking tourists going there to buy our guide, which seemed a bit ambitious.

DS: Do you have in mind a specific target audience for your guides?

RJ: We do, but I'd probably describe them more in terms of life experience and personality type rather than anything demographic.

ME: We cater for a pretty wide band. I would say most of our readers are travelling independently rather than on a package, though things are so grey now that it's difficult to know the difference. People will use, say, our India book very differently to our Paris or Prague book. It's more a question of making the book fit the destination rather than thinking of one type of traveller you're catering for. We do occasional bits of market research but it's amazing how inconclusive it is. Just as we thought, we sell to all different sorts of people.

DS: What, in your opinion, are the characteristics of good and bad guidebook copy?

ME: I think the main thing is to be able to write an interesting sentence, whether it's describing a monument, or a kind of food, or the local football team. Writing that sentence in a way that engages somebody. People spend an awful lot of time with our books, on long train journeys or whatever, and we feel we should give them something interesting to read. People read through large sections of the books about places that they're not even planning to go to. We want the reading experience to be an enjoyable one.

RJ: And you need to be very concise. Space is at an extraordinary premium in a guide because you're expecting people to buy it and then lug it around the streets of wherever. So you don't want to waste their time with superfluous words. My favourite editing dictum is 'omit superfluous words'. Simple as that. The guidebook is not a platform for any writer to be indulgent.

DS: What do you consider bad copy?

ME: Boring copy, copy that doesn't engage you, copy that hasn't been worked over enough or is sloppy. A guidebook has to have a lot of clarity and the authors must know their left from their right and their north from their south. It's amazing how many you come across who don't. So a good sense of direction is a useful thing too!

RJ: We don't like clichés. People who think they are being creative but who actually come up with pretentious clichés. Examples like 'Opera buffs will love . . .' – that presumption of what people will love and also the use of those sort of tabloid words. You don't have to use a clever word when an ordinary word will do. We don't do brochure copy and easily rumble writers who copy from websites rather than do their own research: the tone is unmistakable. 'Since opening its doors in 2001 this hotel has continued to set the highest standards for luxurious ultra-all-inclusive service.' Well thank you because I can just edit all that out in the flick of a cursor. I also despise those who think they're doing us a favour by overwriting and then invoice us for the extra. It's quite nice to have maybe ten per cent over because copy always shrinks during the edit but any more than that and you're causing us serious problems.

DS: How do you decide on new titles in the series?

ME: We can be sold on a place by a proposal. If somebody sends us an outstanding proposal for a growing travel destination – we've recently been looking at Namibia and Ethiopia – and some sample work that makes us think we'd be proud to publish it, we can be sold on the idea. But we look at the numbers of visitors to a destination to see if it's enough to sustain a guidebook.

RJ: We have many different ways. We track visitor statistics. In-house there are various senior staff who have their opinions and then I'll tend to put it all together with extras like visitor numbers, has anyone else tipped it as a hot destination, do we get the feeling there's a buzz about it? And then we do the sums. Some guides emerge because we have a fantastic editor with a proven track record who's very keen to cover a place – like our guide to Marrakesh. As a company we receive a lot of proposals and I think we've done maybe six that way. But it must fit with our brand and our image.

DS: Are there any areas, either geographical or thematic, that are crying out for a guide?

ME: Probably not geographical. We did a skiing and snowboarding guide for North America recently and we might add one for Europe. We might be doing some activity-type things. It's a growing area. It's not very easy to sell thematic books though, mainly because bookshop travel sections are arranged by country and beyond that there is very limited table space. If a shop doesn't have somewhere obvious to put the book, it's a real battle. We did a lovely Mediterranean wildlife guide some years back but there wasn't really a Mediterranean section to put it in so it just got lost. But even with these practical considerations, there are smaller niches that writers can make a success. I guess the answer is to think of where you enjoy going and check out if there is a guide. If there's nothing on the market, you are in with a chance. That's why I started writing my guide to Greece in 1981.

RJ: I hear research that pinpoints a diversification of titles as the way forward for the travel guide market. But I don't know. It's partly the economics. It would be lovely to be specialist and do, say, an adventure sports guide to Europe but can you honestly send someone to 1,000 adventure destinations to find the best 500? The economics of it terrify me and you probably wouldn't sell that many. That said, there are people who have a great idea or innovative distribution or write for free because they love doing it, so all things are possible.

DS: Is it realistic to expect to make a living from travel writing?

RJ: Yes, but there is a point of diminishing returns where one guidebook company won't want to employ you because you're seen as repeating the same work you've done for another company. There's also a fairly high burn-out rate. When it comes to the third or fourth edition many writers lose their motivation. Nor can guidebooks afford to pay fantastic rates so the money might seem attractive at first when the work is fun, but when it's no longer fun, the rates are no longer attractive! To a degree it's a young person's business – you're keen on travelling, everything stimulates, you're attracted to new experiences. So we often give people their first chance – just because someone's not been published before doesn't mean they can't do the job as well as somebody who's been doing it for years.

ME: It's a minority who can make a decent living. Inevitably for anyone coming into it now, it's very difficult because most of the popular destinations have been covered. If you'd got royalties on the guide for New York or Paris you would be on a very good salary. But if you want to write that book on Namibia, it will pay for you to go and produce it but it won't pay the bills at home.

DS: Finally, any great advice for someone looking to get into the industry?

ME: Money has to be the secondary motivation. If you want to spend a year discovering everything there is to know about Catalunya or India, that must be your main motivation. If you go in to it for that reason, you won't be disappointed because you will be financed through that and, though the research and writing are hard work, it will give a focus to what you're doing and make the whole thing worthwhile.

RJ: Be businesslike about it. People tend to treat travel writing as some sort of Holy Grail. But actually, at the editing end it's like anything else. It's all words and they have to be good and suited to their purpose.

From Book to Booking

*Nick Creagh-Osborne, manager of Notting Hill's
Travel Bookshop, and Sharon Benson and Alex Stewart,
manager and chief buyer for Stanfords in London, talk to
Daniel Smith, giving their insight into the travel book market*

DANIEL SMITH: How do the travel bookshops score over the general bookshops?

NICK CREAGH-OSBORNE: What we try to provide for the traveller is a completely rounded experience – the guides plus everything around the subject that you would want to read. We aim to be the first stop for travellers, wherever they happen to be going, and where people who've been looking for a book for years can come and find it on the shelf.

SHARON BENSON: And at Stanfords we've been doing this for 150 years. We have the suppliers that Borders and Waterstones can only dream of.

ALEX STEWART: I think the chain stores do as good a job as they can within the constraints of the head office-led culture. But there is not the same opportunity for individuals within branches to exercise their own judgement or enthusiasms. Here we have much more scope to take a chance on more unusual titles, products and destinations.

DS: Do you have what you might call a typical customer?

NC-O: We have three categories. First of all there is the local community. Then there are the people who come from far and wide wanting travel books because they know that whatever country they're travelling to, we will have the books here on the shelf. And thirdly, we have an international audience courtesy of the film *Notting Hill*. I hadn't realised it had assumed such an iconic status. That film was the greatest advertising fillip any business could hope to have.

SB: I don't think we do have a typical customer at Stanfords, which is refreshing. You get seventeen-year-olds wearing backpacks and you think they're going to be after an Indian adventure but it turns out they've never travelled before and they just want to go to Barcelona for the weekend. Then you'll get a little old lady asking for a trekking map!

AS: Some customers have a brand-name blinker, but if you can persuade them to get beyond that they'll at least have a look at some of the competition. Quite a lot of brands have a very strong loyalty factor. Customers get used to the style of writing and will go back to the familiar brand but its always useful to have an alternative and reassure them there are other things available.

SB: And lots of people just come in for a browse. Especially in the winter. The armchair travellers or people who want some ideas about where to go. So we have lots of people wandering round and hitting upon destinations.

DS: Have you noticed any distinct trends in recent times, particularly with the travel industry being in a rather nervous state?

NC-O: Well, I'm not sure about it being in a nervous state. Obviously the most extreme example of nerves was September 11. That had an impact but strangely it wasn't that long-lived. There are always factors that turn people away from a particular country but they'll go to another instead. A big influence is the weather – most people will go to India at the end of the year because it's our winter and it's warm there, rather than baking hot or the middle of the monsoon season. Subject to that, in recent months we've had an enormous number of people going to Vietnam and Cambodia. Thailand has been saturated by tourism and because it's a wonderful part of the world, people are now looking for new destinations in that area. Vietnam still has the mystery that Thailand had a few decades ago. Cambodia even more so. I think a lot of people are in search of that genuine experience, seeing how people live before they become too affected by Western culture and tourists.

SB: Things are picking up now but the last two or three years have been quite tough. The majority of our stock is guidebooks. For every ten books we have on a country, one will be dedicated to travel writing but the rest will be guidebooks and maps. From September 11 to the following March was a really bad time and we didn't sell much at all but people will always go on holiday. Long-haul destinations dropped off but short-trip destinations rose in their place. And now people are less worried. There are travel problems but they don't seem to make the same impression. Even when countries are thought to be too risky for travel, people enjoy reading about them.

DS: Is it worthwhile travel writers trying to identify trends in book sales?

SB: Twenty years ago everyone was camping in the English countryside but that doesn't really happen any more. Spain, Italy or France are popular but in another ten years we may be back to the English countryside. Nowadays, people do go further afield to find that travel buzz. Places like Cuba are booming which must have something to do with other parts of the world being so over-run by tourism. Writers can have a good shot at predicting upcoming popular destinations. By looking at sales, you can see that Eastern Europe has gone up in the last two or three years and is going to grow and grow. The same with New Zealand.

DS: The range of travel guides seems to be growing all the time. Are there too many guides on offer?

SB: I think there's a danger of there being too many guidebooks but I don't think it does any harm for there to be a bit of competition between them. And they do offer different things to different customers. The Dorling Kindersley *Eyewitness* guides are great for people who like the whole package thing. And Lonely Planet have got a really big following which I think they understand may now be going against them in a way. If people have travelled a lot and are still looking for something off the beaten track, there's maybe a tendency not to go that Lonely Planet route. So there has been an increase in the popularity of lesser-known publishers, which can only be a good thing.

DS: Alex, you have just had a guide to the great walks of New Zealand published by Trailblazer. So how did you get the commission?

AS: In fact, I pitched a different proposal but they had somebody working on a similar project. They asked for further ideas and this was the one they plumped for. Trailblazer are a small outfit and they don't have a lot of capacity for signing up new authors. But I was persistent!

DS: What did they want in the proposal?

AS: Initially they needed a full break-down and justification for why the book might sell, why the destination was appropriate and why it would fit into their list. Once they'd agreed to it in principle they needed a chapter-by-chapter break-down. It had to be fairly detailed before they'd go near it and then we thrashed out the framework. After that I had pretty much a free rein to write my own book. I wrote the words, took the photographs, drew the maps. It's different to something like Lonely Planet, which is very structured.

DS: Are there many areas where you think, why has no one written about that?

AS: There are but you can argue it's because they are not necessarily commercially viable. There are not many publishers willing to pile money into loss-leader destinations. Reykjavik, which is a cult destination, had a guide published recently and this was something we had been crying out for. There are several European cities which deserve their own books but they haven't yet been done.

NC-O: I'm amazed that Rough Guides are only just getting round to publishing their guide to Sri Lanka. A surprising omission. But there are guides to most destinations, with the exception of places like Algeria, where the foreign office more or less offers a disclaimer for people going there.

DS: Away from guidebooks, which other types of travel writing sell the best?

NC-O: It depends on the particular country and what has already been written about. There are the great travel writers – of the current generation, Colin Thubron, Paul Theroux and Eric Newby come to mind. A lot of people seem to be going to Central Asia at the moment and they might buy Colin Thubron's book on Central Asia or Siberia. If they're going to India they might go for Paul Theroux's *The Great Railway Bazaar*. Other people going to, say, Italy, find that Eric Newby has written two books, *Love and War in the Apennines* and *A Small Place in Italy*, so they'll read them as background to their trip.

Others read travel literature simply for the enjoyment and fascination. We sell a lot of history on countries like Russia, Vietnam and Cambodia – places where the heritage has a great impact on the present. Obviously that's true for all countries but there are certain countries where it is more readily apparent. We sell a lot of histories of Egypt, for instance, because when you visit Egypt what you see in terms of chronology is spread over 3,000 years so its good to have an idea of how all that fits together. We don't sell much history for a country like the USA.

DS: So what's the biggest determining factor in the average customer's choice of book?

SB: Most customer choices are destination orientated. You get the odd one or two authors who are clearly trying to do a Bill Bryson-type book but I think most publishers realise it won't work. So really choice is dictated by where people are going and when. We won't sell lots of books on New Zealand in August because people don't go to New Zealand in August.

NC-O: I suppose you can jump on a bandwagon for a hot new place but I don't get the impression that publishers of travel literature do that much. It's the quality of the writing that is paramount. It's not a case of publishers thinking that nobody has written about Mongolia or the Central Sahara so we'll publish a book on it. By the same token, an excellent book on India wouldn't be turned down because there are so many books on India coming out. It's different with travel guides. The guide market is so competitive that a publisher will look for any edge or lead it can get over its rivals. Bradt publishes guides that are excellent for independent travellers and their speciality is writing the first guide to an emerging destination. For instance, they've recently done one on Kabul that was out as soon as it was safe, or safe-ish.

DS: Being surrounded by travel literature all day, do you still manage to read some of it for pleasure?

NC-O: I have a number of writers I return to, such as Paul Theroux – every time I read one of his books it makes me wish I were abroad somewhere. It's the same with Peter Hopkirk writing on Central Asia.

SB: There are particular authors I like and things that particularly grab me. Controversially, I'm not into the Bill Bryson-type of book. I like Lucy Irvine. More than the style of the writing, if the destination appeals to me then I'll go for it. And she writes about living on a desert island. I like William Dalrymple.

AS: Stand-out authors would be people like William Dalrymple, where you can guarantee it's going to be well written and insightful. In recent times, I thought William Fiennes' *The Snow Geese* was a superb book and he has the potential to be a real old-school travel writer. I suppose there's the 'going round Europe with a domestic appliance' comedy books or the 'living abroad in a renovated property' genre that we've had for three or four years now. Every publisher has one and there's very little new to be said about it but they're still selling.

DS: So how do you judge the quality of travel writing?

NC-O: It's a personal point of view, but I don't enjoy a travelogue that's too much like a diary. You should be interested in whoever is leading you round but you don't want to know too much about them. In a successful travel book, the traveller has to travel as Everyman – not only as himself but as you, the reader. Too much ego in a travel book is a very bad thing. If the presence of the author intrudes unduly, I find it disruptive. And I don't like travellers who are too opinionated. I like writers to be critical and discerning but not to the extent where they are making my mind up for me. I like descriptive writers. Jan Morris is one of my great favourites. Not only do you get a factual description of a place, you also get the sight and the feel and the touch.

SB: Many writers are too serious for their own good. The light touch can be very appealing, as those such as Bill Bryson have proved. The bestseller lists are always headed by the likes of Dave Gorman, Pete McCarthy, Tony Hawks. Very successful but not old-school travel writing in the same way as the likes of Eric Newby or Wilfred Thesiger, although people like Newby remain perennial favourites. And there's been a great uptake for Norman Lewis since his recent death. But there is definitely an element of humour in many of the bestsellers. It makes it a more interesting read.

AS: There is still scope for good destination-led, almost anthropological-type reportage. It would be nice to see a return to that to go with the comedies and the living-abroad titles that are at the forefront of most publishers' lists. We run a book of the month here which is an in-house selection and rarely will a Tony Hawks or a Pete McCarthy-type title make it on to that list because we're on the lookout for something a little unusual. But we're in the happy position of being able to sell the more unusual titles in much greater quantities than your average chain store. In recent months we've had Owen Sheers' *The Dust Diaries*, an unusual mix of fiction, memoir and reportage, recounting his own and his great-great-uncle's travels through Zimbabwe. Also, Patrick Leigh Fermor's

Words of Mercury, and *The Journals of a White Sea Wolf* by Mariusz Wilk, an exposé of life in the Siberian wastelands. It's a fantastically written book but maybe not everyone's first choice for holiday reading!

DS: So what does a travel writer have to do to make his book stand out?

NC-O: Ultimately, it's got to be an interesting read. You could write about the most unattractive, unvisitable place in the world but if you write about it well, you will have a readership. A writer like Paul Theroux or Bill Bryson could be put down into the most God-awful part of the world and write a masterpiece. A lot of reading about travelling is wish-fulfilment. It's something that takes you out of your daily life. A successful travel book has to cater to that.

AS: For the guidebook genre, it's hard work and you need persistence and tenaciousness. And when you come up with an idea, target it to the appropriate publisher and don't be afraid if someone draws red ink all over your proposal. It's not a reason to give up.

SB: There's room for everybody, I think. Travel has increased so much over the last twenty years and if you look at any of the major bookshops, they all have a big travel section.

AS: 2004 is pegged for the resurgence of travel in the aftermath of the wars and disease scares of recent years so we should see an upturn in sales. It's a good time for writers to keep pegging away.

Travel Books Bestsellers 2003

1. *The Road to McCarthy* by Pete McCarthy (Hodder) – 129,400
2. *Sahara* by Michael Palin (Phoenix) – 92,200
3. *Notes from a Small Island* by Bill Bryson (Black Swan) – 62,000
4. *Down Under* by Bill Bryson (Black Swan) – 57,400
5. *The Snow Geese* by William Fiennes (Picador) – 56,600
6. *Dark Star Safari: Overland from Cairo to Cape Town* by Paul Theroux (Penguin) – 52,300
7. *The Art of Travel* by Alain de Botton (Penguin) – 47,000
8. *1001 Days Out with Your Kids* (Parragon) – 45,500
9. *McCarthy's Bar: A Journey of Discovery in Ireland* by Pete McCarthy (Sceptre) – 45,000
10. *Neither Here Nor There: Travels in Europe* by Bill Bryson (Black Swan) – 44,800
11. *Round Ireland With a Fridge* by Tony Hawks (Ebury Press) – 37,100
12. *Lonely Planet: Australia* by Tony Wheeler (Lonely Planet Publications) – 35,000
13. *A Parrot in the Pepper Tree* by Chris Stewart (Sort of Books) – 31,100
14. *Driving Over Lemons: An Optimist in Andalucia* by Chris Stewart (Sort of Books) – 30,900

15. *Do Not Pass Go: From the Old Kent Road to Mayfair* by Tim Moore (Vintage) – 29,800
16. *The Good Pub Guide: 2004* (Ebury Press) – 28,000
17. *Lonely Planet: New Zealand* by Tony Wheeler (Lonely Planet Publications) – 27,500
18. *Bill Bryson African Diary* by Bill Bryson (Doubleday) – 26,800
19. *Join Me* by Danny Wallace (Ebury Press) – 26,400
20. *Gardens of England and Wales: 2003* (National Gardens Scheme) – 26,400
21. *The Good Pub Guide: 2003* (Ebury Press) – 26,100
22. *Lost Continent: Travels in Small Town America* by Bill Bryson (Black Swan) – 25,600
23. *Notes from a Big Country* by Bill Bryson (Black Swan) – 25,500
24. *Lonely Planet: Italy* by Neil Tilbury (Lonely Planet Publications) – 22,800
25. *A Walk in the Woods* by Bill Bryson (Black Swan) – 22,600
26. *Caravan and Camping Britain: 2003* (Automobile Association) – 20,900
27. *A Season with Verona* by Tim Parks (Vintage) – 19,700
28. *Are You Dave Gorman?* by Dave Gorman and Danny Wallace (Ebury Press) – 19,500
29. *The Rough Guide to Spain* by Mark Ellingham and John Fisher (Rough Guides) – 18,200
30. *Eyewitness Top 10 Paris* (Dorling Kindersley) – 17,500

LISTINGS

UK Publishers with Travel Writing Lists

AA Publishing

The Automobile Association, Fanum House, Basingstoke RG21 4EA

☎ 01256 491573   Fax 01256 491974

Email rupert.mitchell@theAA.com

Website www.theAA.com

Managing Director *Stephen Mesquita*
Manager, Publishing *Rupert Mitchell*

Publishes maps, atlases and guidebooks, motoring, travel and leisure.

Absolute Press

Scarborough House, 29 James Street West, Bath BA1 2BT

☎ 01225 316013   Fax 01225 445836

Email sales@absolutepress.demon.co.uk

Website www.absolutepress.demon.co.uk

Managing/Editorial Director *Jon Croft*

FOUNDED 1979. Publishes food and wine-related subjects as well as travel guides. No unsolicited mss. Synopses and ideas for books welcome.

Advance Publishing
2 Northumbria Close, Haddenham, Ely CB6 3HT
☎ 01353 7494904
Email editors@advance-publishing.co.uk
Website www.advance-publishing.co.uk

Senior Editor *Julie Underwood*
Editor *Margaret Burrows*

FOUNDED 2002. Publishes non-ficton, fiction, biography, autobiography, history, humour, science fiction, travel, war and crime. Unsolicited mss and synopses considered if accompanied by return postage.

Chris Andrews Publications
15 Curtis Yard, North Hinksey Lane, Oxford OX2 OLX
☎ 01865 723404   Fax 01865 725294
Email chris.andrews1@btclick.com
Website www.cap-ox.co.uk

Managing Director *Chris Andrews*

FOUNDED 1982. Publishes coffee table scenic travel guides. Also calendars, diaries, cards and posters. TITLES *Romance of Oxford; Romance of the Cotswolds; Romance of the Thames & Chilterns.* Unsolicited synopses and ideas for travel/guide books will be considered; phone in the first instance.

Arcadia Books
15–16 Nassau Street, London W1W 7AB
☎ 020 7436 9898   Fax 020 7436 9898
Email info@arcadiabooks.co.uk
Website www.arcadiabooks.co.uk

Managing Director *Gary Pulsifer*
Publishing Director *Daniela de Groote*

Small, independent publishing house, founded in 1996, specialising in translated fiction from around the world. Winner of the **Sunday Times Small Publisher of the Year Award** 2002–03. Publishes literary fiction, gay fiction, biography, autobiography, gender studies, travel writing. Does not welcome unsolicited material.

Aurum Press Ltd
25 Bedford Avenue, London WC1B 3AT
☎ 020 7637 3225   Fax 020 7580 2469
Email editorial@aurumpress.co.uk

Managing Director *Bill McCreadie*
Editorial Director *Piers Burnett*
Approx. Annual Turnover £3 million

FOUNDED 1976. Committed to producing high-quality, illustrated/non-illustrated adult non-fiction in the areas of general human interest, art and craft, lifestyle, sport and travel. IMPRINTS **Argentum** Practical photography books; **Jacqui Small** High-quality lifestyle books.

Berlitz Publishing
58 Borough High Stret, London SE1 1XF
☎ 020 7403 0284   Fax 020 7403 0290
Email publishing@berlitz.co.uk
Website www.berlitz.com

Managing Director *Jeremy Westwood*

FOUNDED 1970. Acquired by the Langenscheidt Publishing Group in February 2002. Publishes travel and language-learning products only: visual travel guides, phrasebooks and language courses. SERIES *Pocket Guides; Berlitz Complete Guide to Cruising and Cruise Ships; Phrase Books; Pocket Dictionaries; Business Phrase Books; Self-teach: Rush Hour Commuter Cassettes; Think & Talk; Berlitz Kids*. No unsolicited mss.

A.&C. Black Publishers Ltd

Alderman House, 37 Soho Square, London W1D 3QZ

☎ 020 7758 0200   Fax 020 7758 0222

Email enquiries@acblack.com

Website www.acblack.com

Chairman *Nigel Newton*
Managing Director *Jill Coleman*
Publishing Director, Reference *Jonathan Glasspool*
Approx. Annual Turnover £10.5 million

Publishes children's and educational books, including music, for 3–15-year-olds, arts and crafts, ceramics, fishing, ornithology, nautical, reference, sport, theatre and travel. Acquisitions brought the Herbert Press' art, design and general books, Adlard Coles' and Thomas Reed's sailing lists, plus *Reed's Nautical Almanac*, Christopher Helm, Pica Press and T&AD Poyser's natural history and ornithology lists into A.&C. Black's stable. Bought by **Bloomsbury Publishing** in May 2000. Owns *Whitaker's Almanack* and children's publisher Andrew Brodie Publications. IMPRINTS **Adlard Coles Nautical; Christopher Helm; The Herbert Press; Pica Press.** TITLES *Who's Who; Writers' & Artists' Yearbook; Know the Game* sports series; *Blue Guides* travel series; *Rockets* and *Black Cats* children's series. Initial enquiry appreciated before submission of mss.

Bradt Travel Guides

19 High Street, Chalfont St Peter SL9 9QE

☎ 01753 893444   Fax 01753 892333

Email info@bradt-travelguides.com

Website www.bradt-travelguides.com

Managing Director *Hilary Bradt*
Editorial Head *Tricia Hayne*
Approx. Annual Turnover £550,000

FOUNDED in 1974 by Hilary Bradt. Specialises in travel guides to off-beat places. SERIES country guides and island guides (Azores, Falklands, St

Helena); wildlife guides (Galapagos, Arctic, Antarctica, Southern Africa); mini guides to cities (Kabul, Baghdad, Lille) and the 'Eccentric' series (Britain, London, France, America). No unsolicited mss; synopses and ideas for travel guidebooks (not travelogues) welcome.

Nicholas Brealey Publishing

3–5 Spafield Street, London EC1R 4QB
☎ 020 7239 0360   Fax 020 7239 0370
Email rights@nbrealey-books.com
Website www.nbrealey-books.com

Managing Director *Nicholas Brealey*

FOUNDED 1992. Independent publishing group focusing on innovative trade/professional books covering business and finance, intelligent self-help, popular psychology and the increasingly active fields of crossing cultures and travel writing. The group now includes Intercultural Press Inc and has a global reach. TITLES *Shackleton's Way; Almost French; 50 Self-Help Classics; Money for Nothing; Authentic Happiness; The 80/20 Principle.* No fiction, poetry or leisure titles. No unsolicited mss; synopses and ideas welcome.

Business Education Publishers Ltd

The Teleport, Doxford International, Sunderland SR3 3XD
☎ 0191 525 2410
Email info@bepl.com
Website www.bepl.com

Managing Director *Mrs A. Murphy*
Approx. Annual Turnover £400,000

FOUNDED 1981. Publishes business education, economics and law for BTEC and GNVQ reading. Currently expanding into further and higher education, computing, IT, business, travel and tourism, occasional papers for institutions and local government administration. Unsolicited mss and synopses welcome.

Cadogan Guides

Highlands House, 165 The Broadway, Wimbledon, London
SW19 1NE
☎ 020 8544 8051   Fax 020 8544 8081
Email info@cadoganguides.co.uk
Website www.cadoganguides.com

Managing Director *Jenny Calcutt*
Managing Editor *Natalie Pomier*

FOUNDED 1982. Travel publisher: country, regional and city guides; parent travel guides (*Take the Kids*); guides to living, working and buying property abroad. Also publishes some travel literature. Most titles are commissioned. No unsolicited material.

Chrysalis Books Group

The Chrysalis Building, Bramley Road, London W10 6SP
☎ 020 7314 1400
Email firstinitialsurname@chrysalisbooks.co.uk
Website www.chrysalisbooks.co.uk

CEO *Marcus Leaver*
Approx. Annual Turnover £33.9 million

Chrysalis Books Group, owned by Chrysalis Group Plc, specialises in illustrated non-fiction, publishing under the IMPRINTS **B.T. Batsford; Brassey's; C&B (Collins & Brown); Conway Maritime Press; Paper Tiger; Pavilion; Putnam Aeronautical Books; Robson Books; Salamander.** IMPRINTS **B.T. Batsford** Publisher *Roger Huggins*. FOUNDED in 1843 as a bookseller, and began publishing in 1874. Acquired by Chrysalis in 1999. A world leader in books on chess, arts and craft. Publishes non-fiction, architecture, heritage, bridge and chess, film and entertainment, fashion, crafts and hobbies. About 100 titles a year. **Brassey's** Publisher *John Lee*. Acquired by Chrysalis in 1999. Publishes military history and technology. **C&B (Collins & Brown)** Publisher *Will Steeds*. Publishes a range of lifestyle categories especially in the areas of practical art, photography and needlecrafts. **Conway Maritime Press** Publisher *John Lee.* Publishes naval history, maritime culture and ship modelling. **Paper Tiger** Publisher *Will Steeds.* Acquired by Chrysalis in 2001 (part of C&B). Publishes science fiction and fantasy art. **Pavilion Books** Editorial Director *Kate Oldfield.* Acquired by Chrysalis in 2001. Publishes illustrated books in biography, cookery, gardening, humour, art, interiors, music, sport and travel. Unsolicited mss not welcome. Ideas and synopses for non-fiction titles considered. **Putnam Aeronautical Books** Publisher *John Lee.* Publishes classic aeronautical histories, technical and reference. **Robson Books** Publisher *Jeremy Robson.* FOUNDED 1973. Acquired by Chrysalis in 1998. Publishes general non-fiction including biography, cookery, gardening, sport and travel. About 90 titles a year. Unsolicited synopses and ideas for books welcome (s.a.e. essential for reply). **Salamander** Publisher *Jo Messham.* FOUNDED 1973. Publishes colour illustrated books on collecting, cookery, interiors, gardening, music, crafts, military, aviation, sport and transport. Also a wide range of books on American interest subjects. No unsolicited mss but synopses and ideas for the above subjects welcome.

Thomas Cook Publishing

PO Box 227, Peterborough PE3 8xx

☎ 01733 417352   Fax 01733 416688

Head of Publishing *Donald Greig*

Approx. Annual Turnover £4 million

Part of the Thomas Cook Group Ltd, publishing commenced in 1873 with the first issue of *Cook's Continental Timetable.* Publishes guidebooks, maps and timetables. No unsolicited mss; synopses and ideas welcome as long as they are travel-related.

Dalesman Publishing Co. Ltd

Stable Courtyard, Broughton Hall, Skipton BD23 3AZ

☎ 01756 701381   Fax 01756 701326

Email editorial@dalesman.co.uk

Website www.dalesman.co.uk

73

Editor *Terry Fletcher*

Publishers of *Dalesman*, *Cumbria and Lake District* and *Peak District* magazines, and regional books covering Yorkshire, the Lake District and the Peak District. Subjects include crafts and hobbies, geography and geology, guidebooks, history and antiquarian, humour, travel and topography. Will consider mss on subjects listed above.

Dorling Kindersley Ltd

Part of the Penguin Group, 80 Strand, London WC2R ORL

☎ 020 7010 3000   Fax 020 7010 6060

Website www.dk.com

Chief Executive *Anthony Forbes Watson*
Managing Director *Andrew Welham*
Publisher *Christopher Davis*

FOUNDED 1974. Packager and publisher of illustrated non-fiction: cookery, crafts, gardening, health, travel guides, atlases, natural history and children's information and fiction. Launched a US imprint in 1991 and an Australian imprint in 1997. Acquired Henderson Publishing in 1995 and was purchased by Pearson plc for £311 million in 2000. DIVISIONS Adult: **Travel/Reference** Publisher *Douglas Amrine*; **General/Lifestyle** Publisher *John Roberts*. Children's: **Reference** Publisher *Miriam Farby*; **PreSchool/Primary** Publisher *Sophie Mitchell*. IMPRINTS **Ladybird**; **Ladybird Audio**; **Funfax**; **Eyewitness Guides**; **Eyewitness Travel Guides**. Unsolicited synopses/ideas for books welcome.

Duncan Petersen Publishing Limited

31 Ceylon Road, London W14 0PY

☎ 020 7371 2356   Fax 020 7371 2507

Email dp@macunlimited.net

Director *Andrew Duncan*

FOUNDED 1986. Publisher and packager of childcare, business, antiques, birds, nature, atlases, walking and travel books. IMPRINT **Duncan Petersen**

SERIES *Charming Small Hotel Guides*; *Charming Restaurant Guides*; *On Foot* (city walking guides). Unsolicited synopses and ideas for books welcome.

Eland Publishing Ltd
Third Floor, 61 Exmouth Market, London EC1R 4QL
☎ 020 7833 0762   Fax 020 7833 4434
Email info@travelbooks.co.uk
Website www.travelbooks.co.uk

Directors *Rose Baring, John Hatt, Barnaby Rogerson*
Approx. Annual Turnover £250,000

Travel reprint specialist, first established by travel writer and editor John Hatt in 1982. Backlist of 60 titles of classic world travel literature. TITLES *Naples '44* Norman Lewis; *Travels with Myself and Another* Martha Gelhorn. IMPRINTS **Sickle Moon** Explorer narratives, history and anthropology. TITLES *Turkish Letters* Busbecq; *The Tuareg* Jeremy Keenan. **Baring & Rogerson** *Poetry of Place* pocket books. No unsolicited mss. Postcards and emails welcome.

Everyman's Library
Northburgh House, 10 Northburgh Street, London EC1V 0AT
☎ 020 7566 6350   Fax 020 7490 3708
Email katy@everyman.uk.com

Publisher *David Campbell*
Approx. Annual Turnover £3.5 million

ESTABLISHED 1906. Publishes hardback classics of world literature, pocket poetry anthologies, children's books and travel guides. Publishes no new titles apart from poetry anthologies; only classics (no new authors). AUTHORS include Bulgakov, Bellow, Borges, Heller, García Márquez, Nabokov, Naipaul, Orwell, Rushdie, Updike, Waugh and Wodehouse. No unsolicited mss.

Foulsham Publishers
The Publishing House, Bennetts Close, Slough SL1 5AP
☎ 01753 526769   Fax 01753 535003

Chairman/Managing Director *B.A.R. Belasco*
Approx. Annual Turnover £2.5 million

FOUNDED 1819 and now one of the few remaining independent family companies to survive takeover. Publishes non-fiction on most subjects including lifestyle, travel guides, family reference, cookery, diet, health, DIY, business, self improvement, self development, astrology, dreams, MBS. No fiction. TITLES *A Brit's Guide to Orlando and Walt Disney World 2002; Old Moore's Almanack.* Unsolicited mss, synopses and ideas welcome.

Fourth Estate Ltd
77–85 Fulham Palace Road, London w6 8jB
☎ 020 8741 4414   Fax 020 8307 4466
Email general@4thestate.co.uk
Website www.4thestate.co.uk

Publishing Director *Nick Pearson*
Editorial Director *Courtney Hodell*
Approx. Annual Turnover £17 million

FOUNDED 1984. Acquired by **HarperCollins** in July 2000, Fourth Estate has a strong reputation for literary fiction and up-to-the-minute non-fiction. Publishes fiction, popular science, current affairs, biography, humour, travel, reference. No unsolicited mss.

Garnet Publishing Ltd
8 Southern Court, South Street, Reading RG1 4QS
☎ 0118 959 7847   Fax 0118 959 7356
Email emma@garnet-ithaca.demon.co.uk
Website www.garnet-ithaca.co.uk

Editorial Manager *Emma G. Hawker*

FOUNDED 1992 and purchased Ithaca Press in the same year. Publishes art, architecture, photography, archive photography, cookery, travel classics, travel, comparative religion, Islamic culture and history, foreign fiction in translation. Core subjects are Middle Eastern but list is rapidly expanding to be more general. IMPRINTS **Garnet Publishing** TITLES *Simply Lebanese; The Story of Islamic Architecture; Traditional Greek Cooking.* **Ithaca Press** Specialises in post-graduate academic works on the Middle East, political science and international relations. TITLES *The Making of the Modern Gulf States; The Palestinian Exodus; French Imperialism in Syria; Philby of Arabia.* Unsolicited mss not welcome – write with outline and ideas first plus current c.v.

Hodder Headline Ltd

338 Euston Road, London NW1 3BH

☎ 020 7873 6000   Fax 020 7873 6024

Website www.hodderheadline.co.uk

Group Chief Executive *Tim Hely Hutchinson*

Approx. Annual Turnover £130 million

Formed in June 1993 through the merger of Headline Book Publishing and Hodder & Stoughton. Headline was formed in 1986 and had grown dramatically, whereas Hodder & Stoughton was 125 years old with a diverse range of publishing. The company was acquired by WHSmith plc in 1999. Purchased **John Murray (Publishers) Ltd** in 2002. DIVISIONS **Headline Book Publishing** Managing Director *Martin Neild*; Deputy Managing Director *Kerr MacRae*; Director of Non-fiction *Val Hudson*; Director of Fiction *Jane Morpeth*. Publishes commercial and literary fiction (hardback and paperback) and popular non-fiction including autobiography, biography, food and wine, gardening, history, popular science, sport and TV tie-ins. **Hodder & Stoughton General** Managing Director *Jamie Hodder-Williams*; **Non-fiction** *Rowena Webb*; **Sceptre** *Carole Welch*; **Audio** (See entry under **Audio Books**). Publishes commercial and literary fiction; biography, autobiography, history, self-help, humour, travel and other general interest non-fiction; audio. **Hodder Children's Books** Managing Director *Charles*

77

Nettleton. **Hodder & Stoughton Religious** Managing Director *Charles Nettleton*; Publishing Director *Judith Longman*; Bibles & Hodder Christian Books *David Moloney*. Publishes NIV Bibles, Christian books, autobiography, TV-tie-ins, gift books, self-help. **Hodder Education** Managing Director *Philip Walters*

Jarrold Publishing

Whitefriars, Norwich NR3 1JR

☎ 01603 763300   Fax 01603 662748

Email info@jarrold-publishing.co.uk

Website www.jarrold-publishing.co.uk

Managing Director *Margot Russell-King*

Part of Jarrold & Sons Ltd, the printing and publishing company founded in 1770. Publishes UK tourism, travel, leisure, history and calendars. Material tends to be of a high pictorial content. IMPRINTS **Pitkin; Unichrome**. Unsolicited mss, synopses and ideas welcome but before submitting anything, approach in writing to the editorial department.

Landmark Publishing Ltd

Ashbourne Hall, Cokayne Avenue, Ashbourne DE6 1EJ

☎ 01335 347349   Fax 01335 347303

Email landmark@clara.net

Website www.landmarkpublishing.co.uk

Chairman *Mr R. Cork*
Managing Director *Mr C.L.M. Porter*
Approx. Annual Turnover £450,000

FOUNDED in 1996. Publishes itinerary-based travel guides, regional, industrial and local history. No unsolicited mss; telephone in the first instance.

Lonely Planet Publications Ltd

72–82 Rosebery Avenue, London EC1R 4RW

☎ 020 7841 9000   Fax 020 7841 9001

Email go@lonelyplanet.co.uk
Website www.lonelyplanet.com

Owner *Lonely Planet (Australia)*
Editorial Head *Katharine Leck*
Approx. Annual Turnover £30 million

FOUNDED in 1973 by Tony and Maureen Wheeler to document a journey from London across Asia to Australia. Since then, Lonely Planet has grown into a global operation with headquarters in Melbourne and offices in Paris, California and London. Publishes travel guidebooks, phrasebooks, travel literature, pictorial books, city maps, regional atlases, diving and snorkelling, walking, cycling, wildlife, health, and pre-departure guidebooks. Also operates a commercial travel slide library called **Lonely Planet Images** (www.lonelyplanetimages.com). No unsolicited mss; synopses and ideas welcome.

Methuen Publishing Ltd

215 Vauxhall Bridge Road, London SW1V 1EJ
☎ 020 7798 1600   Fax 020 7233 9827
Email name@methuen.co.uk
Website www.methuen.co.uk

Managing Director *Peter Tummons*
Publishing Consultant (Methuen) *Max Eilenberg*
Publishing Consultant (Politico's) *Sean Magee*

FOUNDED 1889. Methuen was owned by Reed International until it was bought by Random House in 1997. Purchased by a management buy-out team in 1998. Publishes fiction and non-fiction; travel, sport, drama, film, performing arts, humour. No unsolicited mss; synopses and ideas welcome. Prefers to be approached via agents or a letter of inquiry. No first novels, cookery books, personal memoirs.

Michelin Travel Publications

Hannay House, 39 Clarendon Road, Watford WD17 1JA
☎ 01923 205240   Fax 01923 205241
Website www.Viamichelin.co.uk

FOUNDED 1900 as a travel publisher. Publishes travel guides, maps and atlases. Travel-related synopses and ideas welcome; no mss.

New Holland Publishers (UK) Ltd

Garfield House, 86–88 Edgware Road, London W2 2EA
☎ 020 7724 7773   Fax 020 7258 1293 (editorial)
Email postmaster@nhpub.co.uk
Website www.newhollandpublishers.com

Managing Director *John Beaufoy*
Publishing Managers *Rosemary Wilkinson, Jo Hemmings*
Approx. Annual Turnover £6 million

FOUNDED 1956. Relaunched in 1987 as a publisher of illustrated books for the international market. Publishes non-fiction, practical and inspirational books in categories including cookery and food, crafts, DIY, fishing, gardening, interior design, mind, body and spirit, natural history, indoor and outdoor sports, travel, travel guides and general books. TITLES *The Dating Game; How to Mix and Use Colour; Top Adventure Treks; Container Topiary; One Hit Wonders.* No unsolicited mss; synopses and ideas welcome.

Octagon Press Ltd

PO Box 227, London N6 4EW
☎ 020 8348 9392   Fax 020 8341 5971
Email octagon@schredds.demon.co.uk
Website www.octagonpress.com

Managing Director *George R. Schrager*
Approx. Annual Turnover £100,000

FOUNDED 1972. Publishes philosophy, psychology, travel, Eastern religion, translations of Eastern classics and research monographs in series. Unsolicited material not accepted. Enquiries in writing only.

Quiller Press (An imprint of Quiller Publishing Ltd)

Wykey House, Wykey, Shrewsbury SY4 1JA

☎ 01939 261616   Fax 01939 261606

Email info@quillerbooks.com

Managing Director *Andrew Johnston*

Specialises in sponsored books and publications sold through non-book trade channels as well as bookshops. Publishes architecture, biography, business and industry, collecting, cookery, DIY, gardening, guidebooks, humour, reference, sports, travel, wine and spirits. Most ideas originate in-house; unsolicited mss only if the author sees some potential for sponsorship or guaranteed sales.

The Random House Group Ltd

Random House, 20 Vauxhall Bridge Road, London SW1V 2SA

☎ 020 7840 8400   Fax 020 7233 6058

Email enquiries@randomhouse.co.uk

Website www.randomhouse.co.uk

Chief Executive/Chairman *Gail Rebuck*
Deputy Chairman *Simon Master*
Managing Director *Ian Hudson*

The Random House Group is the UK's leading trade publisher, comprising 31 diverse imprints in four separate substantially autonomous divisions: the Random House Division, Ebury Press, Transworld and Random House Children's Books.

Random House Division IMPRINTS **Jonathan Cape Ltd** ☎ 020 7840 8576   Fax 020 7233 6117 Publishing Director *Dan Franklin* Biography and memoirs, current affairs, fiction, history, photography, poetry, politics and travel. **Yellow Jersey Press; Harvill Secker; Chatto & Windus; Pimlico;**

Vintage ☎020 7840 8573   Fax 020 7233 6117 Publisher *Rachel Cugnoni* Quality paperback fiction and non-fiction. FOUNDED in 1990, Vintage has been described as one of the 'greatest literary success stories in recent British publishing'. **Century** ☎020 7840 8554   Fax 020 7233 6127 Publishing Director *Mark Booth* General fiction and non-fiction including commercial fiction, autobiography, biography, history and self-help. **William Heinemann** ☎020 7840 8400   Fax 020 7233 6127 Publishing Director *Ravi Mirchandani* General non-fiction and fiction, especially history, literary fiction, crime, science, thrillers and women's fiction. **Hutchinson** ☎020 7840 8564   Fax 020 7233 7870 Publishing Director *Sue Freestone* General fiction and non-fiction including notably belles-lettres, current affairs, politics, travel and history. **Random House Business Books** ☎020 7840 8550   Fax 020 7233 6127 Publisher *Clare Smith*. **Arrow** ☎020 7840 8557   Fax 020 7840 6127 Publishing Director *Kate Elton* Mass-market paperback fiction and non-fiction.

EBURY PRESS DIVISION
Tel 020 7840 8400   Fax 020 7840 8406 Publisher *Fiona MacIntyre* IMPRINTS **Ebury Press; Vermilion; Rider; Fodors** Antiques, biography, Buddhism, cookery, gardening, health and beauty, homes and interiors, personal development, spirituality, travel and guides, sport, TV tie-ins.
RANDOM HOUSE CHILDREN'S BOOKS (at Transworld Publishers, 61–63 Uxbridge Road, London W5 5SA   ☎020 8231 6800   Fax 020 8231 6767) Managing Director *Philippa Dickinson*.
Unsolicited mss, synopses and ideas for books welcome.

Reader's Digest Association Ltd
11 Westferry Circus, Canary Wharf, London E14 4HE
☎020 7715 8000   Fax 020 7715 8181
Email gbeditorial@readersdigest.co.uk
Website www.readersdigest.co.uk

Managing Director *Andrew Lynam-Smith*
Editorial Head *Cortina Butler*

Editorial office in the USA. Publishes gardening, natural history, cookery, history, DIY, travel and word books.

Reaktion Books

79 Farringdon Road, London EC1M 3JU

☎ 020 7404 9930   Fax 020 7404 9931

Email info@reaktionbooks.co.uk

Website www.reaktionbooks.co.uk

Managing Director *Michael R. Leaman*

FOUNDED in Edinburgh in 1985 and moved to London in 1987. Publishes art history, architecture, Asian studies, cultural studies, design, film, geography, history, photography and travel writing (*not* travel guides).

SB Publications

19 Grove Road, Seaford BN25 1TP

☎ 01323 893498   Fax 01323 893860

Email sbpublications@tiscali.co.uk

Website www.sbpublications.co.uk

Owner *Mrs Lindsay Woods*

FOUNDED 1987. Specialises in local history, including themes illustrated by old picture postcards and photographs; also travel, guides (town, walking) and railways. TITLES *Dorset As She Wus Spoke; The Neat and Nippy Guide to Brighton; Pre-Raphaelite Trail in Sussex.* Also provides marketing and distribution services for local authors.

Sheldrake Press

188 Cavendish Road, London SW12 0DA

☎ 020 8675 1767   Fax 020 8675 7736

Email mail@sheldrakepress.demon.co.uk

Website www.sheldrakepress.demon.co.uk

Publisher *Simon Rigge*

FOUNDED in 1979 as a book packager and commenced publishing under its own imprint in 1991. Publishes illustrated non-fiction: history, travel, style, cookery and stationery. TITLES *Wild Britain; Wild France; Wild Spain; Wild Italy; Wild Ireland; Amsterdam: Portrait of a City.* Synopses and ideas for books welcome, but not interested in fiction.

Snowbooks Ltd
239 Old Street, London EC1V 9EY
☎ 020 7553 4473   Fax 020 7251 3130
Email editor@snowbooks.com
Website www.snowbooks.com

Managing Director *Emma Cahill*
Approx. Annual Turnover £200,000

FOUNDED 2003. Publishes fiction mainly (both contemporary and classic) but also considers fiction and poetry, non-fiction, humour, children's, business, crime, mystery, travel, general interest, biography and autobiography. Unsolicited synopses and ideas for books welcome provided a sample of writing is attached. Approach by email in the first instance.

Summersdale Publishers Ltd
46 West Street, Chichester PO19 1RP
☎ 01243 771107   Fax 01243 786300
Email submissions@summersdale.com
Website www.summersdale.com

Directors *Stewart Ferris, Alastair Williams*
Commissioning Editor *Sadie Mayne*
Approx. Annual Turnover £1 million

FOUNDED 1990. Publishes travel literature, martial arts, self-help, cookery, humour and gift books. TITLES *Greece on my Wheels* Edward Enfield; *Viva Mallorca* Peter Kerr; *UK on a G-String* Justin Brown. No unsolicited mss; synopses and ideas welcome by email.

I.B.Tauris & Co. Ltd

6 Salem Road, London W2 4BU
☎ 020 7243 1225   Fax 020 7243 1226
Email mail@ibtauris.com
Website www.ibtauris.com

Chairman/Publisher *Iradj Bagherzade*
Managing Director *Jonathan McDonnell*

FOUNDED 1984. Independent publisher. Publishes general non-fiction and academic in the fields of international relations, religion, current affairs, history, politics, cultural, media and film studies, Middle East studies. Joint projects with Cambridge University Centre for Middle Eastern Studies, Institute for Latin American Studies and Institute of Ismaili Studies. *Distributes* Philip Wilson Publishers worldwide. IMPRINTS **Tauris Parke Books** Illustrated books on architecture, travel, design and culture. **Tauris Parke Paperbacks** Trade titles, including art and art history. **British Academic Press** Academic monographs. **Radcliffe Press** Colonial history and biography. Unsolicited synopses and book proposals welcome.

Thames and Hudson Ltd

181A High Holborn, London WC1V 7QX
☎ 020 7845 5000   Fax 020 7845 5050
Email mail@thameshudson.co.uk
Website www.thamesandhudson.com

Managing Director *Thomas Neurath*
Editorial Head *Jamie Camplin*
Approx. Annual Turnover £25 million

Publishes art, archaeology, architecture and design, biography, fashion, garden and landscape design, graphics, history, illustrated and fine editions, mythology, photography, popular culture, style, travel and topography. SERIES *World of Art; New Horizons; Most Beautiful Villages; Earth From the Air.* TITLES *Germaine Greer's The Boy; Manolo Blahnik Drawings; David Hockney: Secret Knowledge; Sensation; The Shock of the New; The Book of Kells;*

Brick: A World History; The Way We Live; The Mind in the Cave; The Eco-Design Handbook; The Seventy Mysteries of Ancient Egypt; The Complete Roman Army; The Mediterranean in History. Send preliminary letter and outline before mss.

Time Warner Books UK

Brettenham House, Lancaster Place, London WC2E 7EN

☎ 020 7911 8000   Fax 020 7911 8100

Email uk@twbg.co.uk

Website www.TimeWarnerBooks.co.uk

Chief Executive *David Young*
Publisher *Ursula Mackenzie*
Approx. Annual Turnover £40 million

FOUNDED 1988 as Little, Brown & Co. (UK). Part of Time Warner. Began by importing its US parent company's titles and in 1990 launched its own illustrated non-fiction list. Two years later the company took over former Macdonald & Co. Publishes hardback and paperback fiction, literary fiction, crime, science fiction and fantasy, and general non-fiction including true crime, biography and autobiography, cinema, gardening, history, humour, popular science, travel, reference, cookery, wines and spirits. IMPRINTS **Little, Brown** *Ursula Mackenzie, Richard Beswick, Barbara Daniel, Hilary Hale, Tara Lawrence* Hardback fiction and general non-fiction. Approach in writing in the first instance. No unsolicited mss.

Travel Publishing Ltd

7A Apollo House, Calleva Park, Aldermaston RG7 8TN

☎ 0118 981 7777   Fax 0118 982 0077

Email info:travelpublishing.co.uk

Website www.travelpublishing.co.uk

Directors *Peter Robinson, Chris Day*

FOUNDED in 1997 by two former directors of **Reed Elsevier plc**. Publishes travel, accommodation, food, drink and specialist shops guides to Britain and Ireland. SERIES **Hidden Places; Hidden Inns; Country Living Rural Guides** (in conjunction with *Country Living* magazine; **Golfers Guides; Off the Motorway**. Welcomes unsolicited material; send letter in the first instance.

Trident Press Ltd
Empire House, 175 Piccadilly, London W1J 9TB
☎020 7491 8770   Fax 020 7491 8664
Email admin@tridentpress.com
Website www.tridentpress.com

Managing Director *Peter Vine*
Approx. Annual Turnover £550,000

FOUNDED 1997. Publishes TV tie-ins, natural history, travel, geography, underwater/marine life, history, archaeology, culture and fiction. DIVISIONS **Fiction/General Publishing** *Paula Vine;* **Natural History** Peter Vine. TITLES *Red Sea Sharks; The Elysium Testament; BBC Wildlife Specials; UAE in Focus.* No unsolicited mss; synopses and ideas welcome, particularly TV tie-ins. Approach in writing or *brief* communications by email, fax or telephone.

UK Literary Agents
for Travel Writers

* = Member of the Association of Authors' Agents

Lorella Belli Literary Agency (LBLA)*

54 Hartford House, 35 Tavistock Crescent, Notting Hill, London
W11 1AY

☎ 020 7727 8547   Fax 0870 787 4194

Email info@lorellabelliagency.com

Website www.lorellabelliagency.com

Contact *Lorella Belli*

FOUNDED 2002. Handles full length fiction (from literary to genre) and
general non-fiction. Particularly interested in first novelists, journalists,
multi-cultural and international writing, books on or about Italy and/or in
Italian. No children's, fantasy, science fiction, poetry, plays or academic
books. CLIENTS include Sean Bidder, Zöe Brân, Scott Capurro, Annalisa
Coppolaro-Nowell, Sean Coughlan, Nino Filastò, Dario Fo (winner of the
1997 Nobel Prize for Literature), Jacopo Fo, Emily Giffin, Paul Martin,
Nisha Minhas, Rupert Steiner, Marcello Vannucci, Diana Winston. *Commission* Home 15%; US & Translation 20%. Works in conjunction with leading
associate agencies in most countries. *Represents* The Imprint Agency (New
York), Studio Nabu Literary Agency (Italy) and Norris Literary Agency,
LLC (Seattle). Welcomes approaches from new authors. Send outline plus

two chapters for non-fiction, and short synopsis plus first thee chapters for fiction. S.a.e. essential. No reading fee. Revision suggested where appropriate.

Juliet Burton Literary Agency

2 Clifton Avenue, London W12 9DR

☎ 020 8762 0148   Fax 020 8743 8765

Email julietburton@virgin.net

Contact *Juliet Burton*

FOUNDED 1999. Handles fiction and non-fiction. Special interests crime and women's fiction. No plays, film scripts, articles, poetry or academic material. *Commission* Home 10%; US & Translation 20%. Approach in writing in the first instance; send synopsis and two sample chapters with s.a.e. No email submissions. No unsolicited mss. No reading fee.

Caroline Davidson Literary Agency

5 Queen Anne's Gardens, London W4 1TU

☎ 020 8995 5768   Fax 020 8994 2770

Contact *Caroline Davidson*

FOUNDED 1988. Handles fiction and non-fiction, including archaeology, architecture, art, astronomy, biography, design, gardening, health, history, medicine, natural history, reference, science. CLIENTS Peter Barham, Nigel Barlow, Andrew Dalby, Emma Donoghue, Cindy Engel, Chris Greenhalgh, Tom Jaine, Huon Mallalieu, Bry Sharma, Linda Sonntag. *Commission* US, Home, Commonwealth, Translation 12½%; 20% if sub-agents are involved. Finished, polished first novels positively welcomed. No occult, short stories, children's, plays or poetry. Writers should send an initial letter giving details of their project and/or book proposal, including the first 50 pages of their novel if a fiction writer, together with c.v. and s.a.e. Submissions without the latter are not considered or returned.

Annette Green Authors' Agency*

1 East Cliff Road, Tunbridge Wells TN4 9AD

☎ 01892 514275   Fax 01892 518124

Email annettekgreen@aol.com

Website www.annettegreenagency.co.uk

Contact *Address material to the Agency*

FOUNDED 1998. Handles literary and general fiction and non-fiction, popular culture and current affairs, science, music, film, history, biography, children's and teenage fiction. No dramatic scripts or poetry. CLIENTS include Andrew Baker, Nick Barlay, Bill Broady, Terry Darlington, Bernie Gaughan, Fiona Gibson, Emma Gold, Justin Hill, Maria McCann, Adam Macqueen, Ian Marchant, Professor Charles Pasternak, Owen Sheers, Elizabeth Woodcraft. *Commission* Home 15%; US & Translation 20%. Letter, synopsis, sample chapters and s.a.e. essential. No reading fee.

International Literary Representation & Management LLC

186 Bickenhall Mansions, Bickenhall Street, London W1U 6BX

☎ 020 7224 1748   Fax 020 7224 1802

Email info@yesitive.com

Website www.yesitive.com

Vice President for Europe *Peter Cox*

European office of US agency. Represents authors with major international potential. CLIENTS Martin Bell, OBE, Brian Clegg, Brian Cruver, Jeff Einstein, Senator Orrin Hatch, Commodore Scott Jones, USN, Josh McHugh, Michael J. Nelson, David Soul, Michelle Paver, Saxon Roach. *Commission* by agreement. Submissions considered only if the guidelines given on the website have been followed. Do not send unsolicited mss by post. No radio or theatre scripts. No reading fee.

Jane Judd Literary Agency*

18 Belitha Villas, London N1 1PD

☎ 020 7607 0273   Fax 020 7607 0623

Contact *Jane Judd*

FOUNDED 1986. Handles general fiction and non-fiction: women's fiction, crime, thrillers, literary fiction, humour, biography, investigative journalism, health, women's interests and travel. 'Looking for good contemporary women's fiction but not Mills & Boon-type.' No scripts, academic, gardening, short stories or DIY. CLIENTS include Andy Dougan, Cliff Goodwin, Jill Mansell, Jonathon Porritt, Rosie Rushton, Manda Scott, David Winner. *Commission* Home 10%; US & Translation 20%. Approach with letter, including synopsis, first chapter and s.a.e. Initial telephone call helpful in the case of non-fiction.

Tamar Karet Literary Agency

56 Priory Road, London N8 7EX
☎ 020 8340 6460   Fax 020 8348 8638
Email tamar.karet.agent@btinternet.com

Contact *Tamar Karet*

Specialises in fiction, travel, leisure, health, cookery, biography, history, social affairs and politics. No academic, children's, poetry, science fiction, horror, militaria or scripts. *Commission* Home 15%; US & Translation 20%. No unsolicited mss; no submissions by email. Send synopsis and sample with s.a.e.

Cat Ledger Literary Agency*

20–21 Newman Street, London W1T 1PG
☎ 020 7861 8226   Fax 020 7861 8001

Contact *Cat Ledger*

FOUNDED 1996. Handles non-fiction: popular culture – film, music, sport, travel, humour, biography, politics; investigative journalism; fiction (non-genre). No scripts. No children's, poetry, fantasy, science fiction, romance. *Commission* Home 10%; US & Translation 20%. No unsolicited mss; approach with preliminary letter, synopsis and s.a.e. No reading fee.

London Independent Books

26 Chalcot Crescent, London NW1 8YD

☎ 020 7706 0486   Fax 020 7724 3122

Proprietor *Carolyn Whitaker*

FOUNDED 1971. A self-styled 'small and idiosyncratic' agency. Handles fiction and non-fiction reflecting the tastes of the proprietor. All subjects considered (except computer books and young children's), providing the treatment is strong and saleable. Scripts handled only if by existing clients. Special interests boats, travel, travelogues, commercial fiction, science fiction and fantasy. *Commission* Home 15%; US & Translation 20%. No unsolicited mss; letter, synopsis and first two chapters with return postage the best approach. No reading fee.

Duncan McAra

28 Beresford Gardens, Edinburgh EH5 3ES

☎ 0131 552 1558   Fax 0131 552 1558

Email duncanmcara@hotmail.com

Contact *Duncan McAra*

FOUNDED 1988. Handles fiction (literary fiction) and non-fiction, including art, architecture, archaeology, biography, military, travel and books of Scottish interest. *Commission* Home 10%; Overseas 20%. Preliminary letter, synopsis and sample chapter (including return postage) essential. No reading fee.

Andrew Mann Ltd*

1 Old Compton Street, London W1D 5JA

☎ 020 7734 4751   Fax 020 7287 9264

Email manscript@onetel.net.uk

Contacts *Anne Dewe, Tina Betts, Sacha Elliot*

FOUNDED 1975. Handles fiction, general non-fiction, children's and film, TV, theatre, radio scripts. *Commission* Home 15%; US & Translation 20%.

Overseas associates various. No unsolicited mss. Preliminary letter, synopsis and s.a.e. essential. Email submissions for synopses only. No reading fee.

John Pawsey
60 High Street, Tarring, Worthing BN14 7NR
☎ 01903 205167   Fax 01903 205167

Contact *John Pawsey*

FOUNDED 1981. Experience in the publishing business has helped to attract some top names here, but the door remains open for bright, new ideas. Handles non-fiction: biography, politics, current affairs, popular culture, travel, sport, business; also fiction: crime, thrillers, suspense but not science fiction, fantasy or horror. Special interests sport and biography. No children's, drama scripts, poetry, short stories, journalism or academic. CLIENTS include David Rayvern Allen, David Ashforth, Jennie Bond, Elwyn Hartley Edwards, William Fotheringham, Don Hale, Patricia Hall, Dr David Lewis, Anne Mustoe. *Commission* Home 12½%; US & Translation 19–25%. *Overseas associates* in the US, Japan, South America and throughout Europe. Preliminary letter with s.a.e. essential. No reading fee.

Pollinger Limited*
9 Staple Inn, London WC1V 7QH
☎ 020 7404 0342   Fax 020 7242 5737
Email info@pollingerltd.com *and* Permissions:
permissions@pollingerltd.com
Website www.pollingerltd.com

Chairman *Paul Woolf*
Managing Director *Lesley Pollinger*
Agents *Lesley Pollinger, Joanna Devereux*
Rights Manager *Katy Loffman*
Consultants *Leigh Pollinger, Joan Deitch*

FOUNDED 2002. A successor of Laurence Pollinger Limited (founded 1958) and Pearn, Pollinger & Higham. Handles all types of general trade adult and children's fiction and non-fiction books; intellectual property development, illustrators/photographers. CLIENTS include Derrry Brabbs, Michael Coleman, Teresa Driscoll, Catherine Fisher, Philip Gross, Catherine Johnson, Gary Latham, Gary Paulsen, Nicholas Rhea and Sue Welford. Also the estates of H.E. Bates, Vera Chapman, Louis Bromfield, Erskine Caldwell, D.H. Lawrence, John Masters, W.H. Robinson, Eric Frank Russell, Clifford D. Simak and other notables. *Commission* Home 15%; Translation 20%. Overseas theatrical, and media associates. No unsolicited material.

Elizabeth Puttick Literary Agency*
46 Brookfield Mansions, Highgate Hill West, London N6 6AT
☎ 020 8340 6383   Fax 0870 751 8098
Email agency@puttick.com
Website www.puttick.com
Contact *Liz Puttick*

FOUNDED 1995. Handles general non-fiction (including illustrated books) with special interest in self-help, mind-body-spirit, health and fitness, lifestyle, business. Also interested in narrative non-fiction, biography, history, philosophy, science, humour, and popular culture. No fiction, poetry, scripts, drama or children's books. CLIENTS include William Bloom, Cornel Chin, Mike Fisher, Ann-Marie Gallagher, Ross Heaven, Nirmala Heriza, Martin Lewis, Steve Nobel, Emma Restall Orr, Ed and Deb Shapiro. *Commission* Home 15%; US & Translation 20%. Works with associates in the US and with the **Marsh Agency** for translation rights. Preliminary enquiries and c.v. by post or email. No reading fee, but s.a.e. essential.

The Sayle Literary Agency*
Bickerton House, 25–27 Bickerton Road, London N19 5JT
☎ 020 7263 8681   Fax 020 7561 0529
Proprietor *Rachel Calder*

Handles fiction, crime and general. Non-fiction: current affairs, social issues, travel, biographies, historical. No plays, poetry, children's, textbooks, technical, legal or medical books. CLIENTS Stephen Amidon, Billy Bragg, Pete Davies, Margaret Forster, Georgina Hammick, Andy Kershaw, Phillip Knightley, Denise Mina, Malcolm Pryce, Kate Pullinger, Ronald Searle, Gitta Sereny, Stanley Stewart, William Styron. *Commission* Home 15%; US & Translation 20%. *Overseas associates* Dunow & Carlson Literary Agency; Darhansoff, Verrill and Feldman; Anne Edelstein Literary Agency; Sally Wofford-Girand Agency; New England Publishing Associates, USA; translation rights handled by **The Marsh Agency**; film rights by **Sayle Screen Ltd**. No unsolicited mss. Preliminary letter essential, including a brief biographical note and a synopsis plus two or three sample chapters. Return postage essential. No reading fee.

Sheil Land Associates Ltd* (incorporating **Richard Scott Simon Ltd 1971** and **Christy Moore Ltd 1912**)
43 Doughty Street, London WC1N 2LH
☎020 7405 9351   Fax 020 7831 2127
Email info@sheilland.co.uk

Agents, UK & US *Sonia Land, Luigi Bonomi, Vivien Green, Amanda Preston*
Film/Theatrical/TV *John Rush, Roland Baggott*
Foreign *Amelia Cummins, Vanessa Forbes*

FOUNDED 1962. Handles full-length general, commercial and literary fiction and non-fiction, including: social politics, business, history, science, military history, gardening, thrillers, crime, romance, drama, biography, travel, cookery and humour, UK and foreign estates. Also theatre, film, radio and TV scripts. CLIENTS include Peter Ackroyd, Hugh Bicheno, Melvyn Bragg, Stephanie Calman, David Cohen, Catherine Cookson estate, Anna del Conte, Seamus Deane, Alan Drury, Erik Durschmied, Alan Garner, Bonnie Greer, Susan Hill, Richard Holmes, HRH The Prince of Wales, John Humphries, Mark Irving, Simon Kernick, James Long, Richard Mabey, Colin McDowell, Patrick O'Brian estate, Esther Rantzen, Pam Rhodes, Jean Rhys estate, Richard and Judy, Martin Riley, Colin Shindler, Tom Sharpe, Martin Stephen, Brian Sykes, Jeffrey Tayler, Alan Titchmarsh, Rose Tremain, Phil Vickery, John Wilsher, Toby Young. *Commission* Home 15%; US

& Translation 20%. *Overseas associates* **Georges Borchardt, Inc.** (Richard Scott Simon). UK representatives for **Farrar, Straus & Giroux, Inc.** US film and TV representation: CAA, APA, and others. Welcomes approaches from new clients either to start or to develop their careers. Preliminary letter with s.a.e. essential. No reading fee.

Sinclair-Stevenson

3 South Terrace, London SW7 2TB

☎ 020 7581 2550   Fax 020 7581 2550

Contact *Christopher Sinclair-Stevenson*

FOUNDED 1995. Handles biography, current affairs, travel, history, fiction, the arts. No scripts, children's, academic, science fiction/fantasy. CLIENTS include Jennifer Johnston, J.D.F. Jones, Ross King, Christopher Lee, Andrew Sinclair and the estates of Alec Guinness, John Cowper Powys and John Galsworthy. *Commission* Home 10%; US 15%; Translation 20%. *Overseas associate* T.C. Wallace Ltd, New York. Translation rights handled by **David Higham Associates**. Send synopsis with s.a.e. in the first instance. No reading fee.

Ed Victor Ltd*

6 Bayley Street, Bedford Square, London WC1B 3HE

☎ 020 7304 4100   Fax 020 7304 4111

Contacts *Ed Victor, Graham Greene, Maggie Phillips, Sophie Hicks, Grainne Fox*

FOUNDED 1976. Handles a broad range of material including children's books but leans towards the more commercial ends of the fiction and non-fiction spectrums. No poetry, scripts or academic. Takes on very few new writers. After trying his hand at book publishing and literary magazines, Ed Victor, an ebullient American, found his true vocation. Strong opinions, very pushy and works hard for those whose intelligence he respects. Loves nothing more than a good title auction. CLIENTS include Eoin Colfer, Frederick Forsyth, A.A. Gill, Josephine Hart, Jack Higgins, Erica Jong,

Nigella Lawson, Kathy Lette, Allan Mallinson, Anne Robinson and the estates of Douglas Adams, Raymond Chandler, Dame Iris Murdoch, Sir Stephen Spender and Irving Wallace. *Commission* Home & US 15%; Translation 20%. No unsolicited mss.

National Newspapers

Departmental email addresses are too numerous to include in this listing. They can be obtained from the newspaper's main switchboard or the department in question.

The Business
292 Vauxhall Bridge Road, London SW1V 1SS
☎ 020 7961 0000

Owner *Barclay Brothers*
Editor-in-Chief *Andrew Neil*
Circulation 282,110

Launched in February 1998. Sunday national newspaper dedicated to business, finance and politics. No unsolicited material. All ideas must be discussed with the department's editor in advance.
Political Editor *Fraser Nelson*

Daily Express
Ludgate House, 245 Blackfriars Road, London SE1 9UX
☎ 020 7928 8000   Fax 020 7620 1654
Website www.express.co.uk

Owner *Northern & Shell Media/Richard Desmond*
Editor *Peter Hill*
Circulation 942,171

Under owner Richard Desmond, publisher of *OK!* magazine, the paper features a large amount of celebrity coverage. The general rule of thumb is to approach in writing with an idea; all departments are prepared to look at an outline without commitment. Ideas welcome but already receives many which are 'too numerous to count'.

News Editor *David Leigh*
Diary (Hickey Column) *Kathryn Spencer*
Features Editor *Heather Preen*
City Editor *Stephen Kahn*
Political Editor *Patrick O'Flynn*
Travel Editor *Jane Memmler*
Planning Editor (News Desk) should be circulated with copies of official reports, press releases, etc., to ensure news desk cover at all times.
Saturday magazine. Editor *Graham Bailey*
Payment negotiable.

Daily Mail

Northcliffe House, 2 Derry Street, London w8 5TT
☎ 020 7938 6000

Owner *Associated Newspapers/Lord Rothermere*
Editor *Paul Dacre*
Circulation 2.4 million

In-house feature writers and regular columnists provide much of the material. Photo-stories and crusading features often appear; it's essential to hit the right note to be a successful *Mail* writer. Close scrutiny of the paper is strongly advised. Not a good bet for the unseasoned. Accepts news on savings, building societies, insurance, unit trusts, legal rights and tax.

News Editor *Tony Gallagher*
City Editor *Alex Brummer*
'Money Mail' Editor *Tony Hazell*
Political Editor *David Hughes*
Education Correspondent *Sarah Harris*
Diary Editor *Richard Kay*

Features Editor *Leaf Kalfayan*
Literary Editor *Jane Mays*
Travel Editor *Mark Palmer*
Femail Lisa Collins
Weekend: Saturday supplement. Editor *Heather McGlone*

Daily Mirror

1 Canada Square, Canary Wharf, London E14 5AP
☎ 020 7293 3000   Fax 020 7293 3409
Website www.mirror.co.uk

Owner *Trinity Mirror plc*
Editor *to be appointed*
Circulation 1.9 million

No freelance opportunities for the inexperienced, but strong writers who understand what the tabloid market demands are always needed.
Deputy Editor *Des Kelly*
News Editor *Conor Hanna*
Features Editor *Peter Willis*
Political Editor *James Hardy*
Business Editor *Clinton Manning*
Showbusiness Diary Editor *Jessica Callan*
Travel Editor *Ian Mayhew*

Daily Record

One Central Quay, Glasgow G3 8DA
☎ 0141 309 3000   Fax 0141 309 3340
Website www.record-mail.co.uk

Owner *Trinity Mirror plc*
Editor *Bruce Waddell*
Circulation 503,077

Mass-market Scottish tabloid.
Freelance material is generally welcome.

News Editor *Tom Hamilton*
Features Editor *Melanie Harvey*
Business Editor *John Penman*
Political Editor *Paul Sinclair*
Associate Sports Editor *Alan Thomson*
Saturday Magazine Editor (including Travel) *Angela Dewar*
Scotland Means Business: Quarterly business magazine, launched March 2002. Editor *Magnus Gardham*

Daily Sport
19 Great Ancoats Street, Manchester M60 4BT
☎ 0161 236 4466   Fax 0161 236 4535
Website www.dailysport.co.uk

Owner *Sport Newspapers Ltd*
Editor *David Beevers*
Circulation 200,000

Tabloid catering for young male readership. Unsolicited material welcome; send to News Editor.
News Editor *Nick Appleyard*
Sports Editor *Marc Smith*
Lads Mag Monthly glossy magazine. Editor *Mark Harris*.

Daily Star
Ludgate House, 245 Blackfriars Road, London SE1 9UX
☎ 020 7928 8000   Fax 020 7922 7960

Owner *Northern & Shell Media/Richard Desmond*
Editor *Dawn Neesom*
Circulation 903,702

In competition with *The Sun* for off-the-wall news and features. Freelance opportunities available.
Deputy Editor *Jim Mansell*

Assistant Editor, Features *Samm Taylor*
Travel Editor *Victoria Lissaman*

Daily Star Sunday
Ludgate House, 245 Blackfriars Road, London SE1 9UX
☎ 020 7928 8000

Owner *Richard Desmond*
Editor *Gareth Morgan*
Circulation 556,751

New Sunday, launched in September 2002 in direct competition with *News of the World* and *The People*.
Travel Editor *Victoria Lissaman*
Supplement: *Hot Celebs*: Showbiz/glamour magazine.

The Daily Telegraph
1 Canada Square, Canary Wharf, London E14 5DT
☎ 020 7538 5000   Fax 020 7513 2506
Website www.telegraph.co.uk

Owner *Sir David and Sir Frederick Barclay*
Editor *Martin Newland*
Circulation 923,042

Unsolicited mss not generally welcome – 'all are carefully read and considered, but very few published'. Contenders should approach the paper in writing, making clear their authority for writing on that subject. No fiction.
Home Editor *Fiona Barton* Tip-offs or news reports from *bona fide* journalists. Must phone the news desk in first instance. Maximum 200 words. Payment minimum £40 (tip).
Arts Editor *Sarah Crompton*
City Editor *Neil Collins*
Political Editor *George Jones*
Diary Editor *Charlie Methvin* Always interested in diary pieces.

Education *John Clare*
Environment *Charles Clover*
Features Editor *Richard Preston* Most material supplied by commission from established contributors. New writers are tried out by arrangement with the features editor. Approach in writing. Maximum 1500 words.
Literary Editor *Kate Summerscale*
Travel Editor *Graham Boynton*
Style Editor *Rachel Forder*
Daily Telegraph Weekend: Saturday supplement. Editor *Michele Lavery*

Financial Times

1 Southwark Bridge, London SE1 9HL
☎ 020 7873 3000   Fax 020 7873 3076
Email firstname.lastname@ft.com
Website www.ft.com

Owner *Pearson*
Editor *Andrew Gowers*
Circulation 448,791

FOUNDED 1888. UK and international coverage of business, finance, politics, technology, management, marketing and the arts. All feature ideas must be discussed with the department's editor in advance. Not snowed under with unsolicited contributions – they get less than any other national newspaper. Approach by email with ideas in the first instance.
News Editor *Edward Carr*
Features Editor *Andrew Hill*
Arts Editor *Lorna Dolan*
Financial Editor *Jane Fuller*
Literary Editor *Jan Dalley*
Diary Editor *Sundeep Tucker*
Education *Miranda Green*
Environment *Vanessa Houlder*
Political Editor *James Blitz*
Travel Editor *Rahul Jacob*

Weekend FT: Editor *Richard Addis*
How to Spend It: Monthly magazine. Editor *Gillian de Bono*

The Guardian
119 Farringdon Road, London EC1R 3ER
☎ 020 7278 2332   Fax 020 7837 2114
Email firstname.secondname@guardian.co.uk
Website www.guardian.co.uk

Owner *The Scott Trust*
Editor *Alan Rusbridger*
Circulation 376,287

Of all the nationals *The Guardian* probably offers the greatest opportunities for freelance writers, if only because it has the greatest number of specialised pages which use freelance work. But mss must be directed at a specific slot.

News Editor *Paul Johnson* No opportunities except in those regions where there is presently no local contact for news stories.

Home News *Ed Pilkington*

Arts Editor *Charlie English*

Literary Editor *Claire Armitstead*

Financial Editor *Paul Murphy*

City Editor *Julia Finch*

Life *Simon Rogers* Thursday supplement, published in association with *Nature*. Science, technology, medicine, environment and other issues. Incorporates *Online* science and computing. Computing/communications (Internet) articles should be addressed to *Jack Schofield*; science articles to *Tim Radford*. Mss on disk or by email (neil.mcintosh@guardian.co.uk).

Diary Editor *Matthew Norman*

Education Editor *Will Woodward* Expert pieces on modern education welcome.

Environment *John Vidal*

Features Editor *Ian Katz* Receives up to 50 unsolicited mss a day; these are passed on to relevant page editors.

Guardian Society *Patrick Butler* Focuses on social change – the forces affecting us, from environment to government policies. Top journalists and outside commentators.

Media Editor *Charlie Burgess* Nine pages a week, plus 'New Media'. Outside contributions are considered. All aspects of modern media, advertising and PR. Background insight important. Best approach is by email (janine.gibson@guardian.co.uk)

Political Editor *Mike White*

Travel Editor *Andy Pietrasik*

Women's Page *Clare Margetson* Runs three days a week. Unsolicited ideas used if they show an appreciation of the page in question. Maximum 800–1000 words. Write, email (clare.margetson@guardian.co.uk) or fax 020 7239 9935.

The Guardian Weekend: Glossy Saturday issue. Editor *Katharine Viner*

The Guide: *Tim Lusher*

The Herald (Glasgow)

200 Renfield Street, Glasgow G2 3PR

☎ 0141 302 7000   Fax 0141 302 7070

Website www.theherald.co.uk

Owner *Gannett UK Ltd*

Editor *Mark Douglas-Home*

Circulation 83,083

One of the oldest national newspapers in the English-speaking world, *The Herald*, which dropped its 'Glasgow' prefix in February 1992, was bought by Scottish Television in 1996. Lively, quality, national Scottish daily broadsheet. Approach with ideas in writing or by phone in the first instance.

News Editor *Magnus Llewelin*

Arts Editor *Keith Bruce*

Business Editor *Ian McConnell*

Diary *Ken Smith*

Education *Liz Buie*

Sports Editor *Donald Cowey*
Herald Magazine *Kathleen Morgan*

The Independent

Independent House, 191 Marsh Wall, London E14 9RS
☎ 020 7005 2000   Fax 020 7005 2999
Website www.independent.co.uk

Owner *Independent Newspapers*
Editor *Simon Kelner*
Circulation 258,012

FOUNDED 1986. Particularly strong on its arts/media coverage, with a high proportion of feature material. Theoretically, opportunities for freelancers are good. However, unsolicited mss are not welcome; most pieces originate in-house or from known and trusted outsiders. Ideas should be submitted in writing.
News Editor *Michael Ellison*
Features *Adam Leigh*
Arts Editor *Ian Irvine*
Business Editor *Jeremy Warner*
Education *Richard Garner*
Environment *Michael McCarthy*
Literary Editor *Boyd Tonkin*
Political Editor *Andrew Grice*
Sports Editor *Paul Newman*
Travel Editor *Simon Calder*
The Independent Magazine: Saturday supplement. Editor *Laurence Earle*
The Independent Traveller: 32-page Saturday magazine
The Information: Editor *Jo Ellison*

Independent on Sunday

Independent House, 191 Marsh Wall, London E14 9RS
☎ 020 7005 2000   Fax 020 7005 2999
Website www.independent.co.uk/sindy/sindy.html

Owner *Independent Newspapers*
Editor *Tristan Davies*
Circulation 209,236

FOUNDED 1986. Regular columnists contribute most material but feature opportunites exist. Approach with ideas in the first instance.
News Editor *Robert Mendick*
Focus Editor *Cole Moreton*
Arts Editor *Marcus Field*
Comment Editor *James Hanning*
Business Editor *Jason Nissé*
Literary Editor *Suzi Feay*
Environment *Geoffrey Lean*
Political Editor *Andy McSmith*
Sports Editor *Neil Morton*
Travel Editor *Kate Simon*
The Sunday Review: supplement. Editor *Andrew Tuck*
ABC: Arts, books and culture supplement.

International Herald Tribune

6 bis, rue des Graviers, 92521 Neuilly, Paris, France
☎ 0033 1 4143 9300   Fax 0033 1 4143 9338 (editorial)
Email iht@iht.com
Website www.iht.com

Executive Editor *Walter Wells*
Deputy Editors *Katherine Knorr, Robert Marino*
Circulation 245,223

Published in France, Monday to Saturday, and circulated in Europe, the Middle East, North Africa, the Far East and the USA. General news, business and financial, arts and leisure. Uses regular freelance contributors. Contributor policy can be found on the website at: www.iht.com/contributor.htm

The Mail on Sunday

Northcliffe House, 2 Derry Street, London w8 5TS

☎ 020 7938 6000   Fax 020 7937 3829

Owner *Associated Newspapers/Lord Rothermere*
Editor *Peter Wright*
Circulation 2.4 million

Sunday paper with a high proportion of newsy features and articles. Experience and judgement required to break into its band of regular feature writers.

News Editor *Sebastian Hamilton*
Financial Editor *Lisa Buckingham*
Diary Editor *Adam Helliker*
Features Editor/Women's Page *Sian James*
Books *Marilyn Warnick*
Political Editor *Simon Walters*
Travel Editor *Frank Barrett*
Night & Day Editor *Christena Appleyard*
Review Editor *Jim Gillespie*
You – The Mail on Sunday Magazine: Colour supplement. Many feature articles, supplied entirely by freelance writers. Editor *Sue Peart*. Features Editor *Rosalind Lowe*

Morning Star

William Rust House, 52 Beachy Road, London E3 2NS

☎ 020 8510 0815   Fax 020 8986 5694

Email morsta@geo2.poptel.org.uk

Owner *Peoples Press Printing Society*
Editor *John Haylett*
Circulation 9000

Not to be confused with the *Daily Star*, the *Morning Star* is the farthest left national daily. Those with a penchant for a Marxist reading of events and ideas can try their luck, though feature space is as competitive here as in the other nationals.

News Editor *Dan Coysh*
Features & Arts Editor *Richard Bagley*
Political Editor *Adrian Roberts*
Foreign Editor *Dave Williams*
Sports Editor *Mark Barber*

News of the World

1 Virginia Street, London E98 1NW
☎ 020 7782 1000   Fax 020 7583 9504
Website www.newsoftheworld.co.uk

Owner *News International plc/Rupert Murdoch*
Editor *Andy Coulson*
Circulation 3.9 million

Highest circulation Sunday paper. Freelance contributions welcome. News and features editors welcome tips and ideas.

Deputy Editor *Neil Wallis*
News Editor *Gary Thompson*
Features Editor *Jules Stenson*
Business/City Editor *Peter Prendergast*
Political Editor *Ian Kirby*
Travel Editor *John Barnsley*
Sunday Magazine: Colour supplement. Editor *Judy McGuire*. Showbiz interviews and strong human-interest features make up most of the content, but there are no strict rules about what is 'interesting'. Unsolicited mss and ideas welcome.

The Observer

119 Farringdon Road, London EC1R 3ER
☎ 020 7278 2332   Fax 020 7713 4250
Email editor@observer.co.uk
Website www.observer.co.uk

Owner *Guardian Newspapers Ltd*
Editor *Roger Alton*
Circulation 452,257

FOUNDED 1791. Acquired by Guardian Newspapers from Lonrho in May 1993. Occupies the middle ground of Sunday newspaper politics.
Unsolicited material is not generally welcome, 'except from distinguished, established writers'. Receives far too many unsolicited offerings already. No news, fiction or special page opportunities. The newspaper runs annual competitions which change from year to year. Details are advertised in the newspaper.
Executive Editor, News *Andy Malone*
Arts Editor *Jane Ferguson*
Review Editor *Louise France*
Comment Editor *Mike Holland*
Deputy Business Editor/City Editor *Richard Wachman*
Business Editor *Frank Kane*
Personal Finance Editor *Maria Scott*
Science Editor *Robin McKie*
Education Editor *Martin Bright*
Environment Correspondent *Mark Townsend*
Literary Editor *Robert McCrum*
Travel Editor *Jeannette Hyde*
Sports Editor *Brian Oliver*
The Observer Magazine: Glossy arts and lifestyle supplement. Editor *Allan Jenkins*
The Observer Sport Monthly: Magazine supplement launched in 2000. *Jason Cowley*
The Observer Food Monthly: Launched in 2001. Editor *Nicola Jeal*
The Observer Music Monthly: Launched in 2003. Editor *Caspar Llewellyn Smith*

The People

1 Canada Square, Canary Wharf, London E14 5AP
☎ 020 7293 3614   Fax 020 7293 3887
Website www.people.co.uk

Owner *Trinity Mirror plc*
Editor *Mark Thomas*
Circulation 1.02 million

Slightly up-market version of *The News of the World*. Keen on exposés and big-name gossip. Interested in ideas for investigative articles. Phone in the first instance.
News Editor *Ian Edmondson*
Features Editor *Rachael Bletchley*
Political Editor *Nigel Nelson*
Sports Editor *Lee Clayton*
Travel Associate Editor *Trisha Harbord*
Take It Easy: Magazine supplement. Editor *Kerry Parnell* Approach by phone with ideas in the first instance.

Scotland on Sunday

Barclay House, 108 Holyrood Road, Edinburgh EH8 8AS
☎ 0131 620 8620   Fax 0131 620 8491
Website www.scotlandonsunday.com

Owner *Scotsman Publications Ltd*
Editor *John McLellan*
Circulation 83,952

Scotland's top-selling quality broadsheet. Welcomes ideas rather than finished articles.
News Editor *Peter Laing*
Features (including Travel) Editor *Sally Raikes*
Arts Editor *Fiona Leith*
Spectrum: Colour supplement. Features on personalities, etc. Editor *Eilidh MacAskill*

The Scotsman

Barclay House, 108 Holyrood Road, Edinburgh EH8 8AS
☎ 0131 620 8620   Fax 0131 620 8616 (Editorial)
Website www.scotsman.com

Owner *Scotsman Publications Ltd*
Editor *Iain Martin*
Circulation 70,656

Scotland's national newspaper. Many unsolicited mss come in, and stand a good chance of being read, although a small army of regulars supply much of the feature material not written in-house. See website for contact details.
News Editor *Nick Drainey*
Business Editor *Nick Bevens*
Education *Seonag MacKinnon*
Features (including Travel) Editor *Clare Trodden*
Book Reviews *David Robinson*
Sports Editor *Donald Walker*

The Sun

1 Virginia Street, London E98 1SN
☎ 020 7782 4000   Fax 020 7782 4108
Email firstname.lastname@the-sun.co.uk
Website www.the-sun.co.uk

Owner *News International plc/Rupert Murdoch*
Editor *Rebekah Wade*
Circulation 3.3 million

Highest circulation daily. Populist outlook; very keen on gossip, pop stars, TV soap, scandals and exposés of all kinds. No room for non-professional feature writers; 'investigative journalism' of a certain hue is always in demand, however.
Head of News *Paul Field*
Head of Features *Graham Dudman*
Head of Sport *Steve Waring*

Woman's Editor *Sharon Hendry*
Travel Editor *Lisa Minot*

Sunday Express

Ludgate House, 245 Blackfriars Road, London SE1 9UX
☎ 020 7928 8000   Fax 020 7620 1654

Owner *Northern & Shell Media/Richard Desmond*
Editor *Martin Townsend*
Circulation 952,171

The general rule of thumb is to approach in writing with an idea; all departments are prepared to look at an outline without commitment.
News Editor *Jim Murray*
Features Editor *Giulia Rhodes*
Business Editor *David Paisley*
Political Editor *Julia Hartley-Brewer*
Travel Editor *Jane Memmler*
S: Fashion and lifestyle magazine for women. Editor *Louise Robinson*. No unsolicited mss. All contributions are commissioned. Ideas in writing only.
S2: News and lifestyle magazine for men. Editor *Phil McNeill*
Payment negotiable.

Sunday Herald

200 Renfield Street, Glasgow G2 3QB
☎ 0141 302 7800   Fax 0141 302 7815
Email editor@sundayherald.com
Website www.sundayherald.com

Owner *Newsquest*
Editor *Andrew Jaspan*
Circulation 58,303

Also at: 9/10 St Andrew Square, Edinburgh EH2 2AF
☎ 0131 718 6040   Fax 0131 718 6105
Launched February 1999. Scottish seven-section broadsheet.

Deputy Editor *Richard Walker*
News Editor *David Milne*
Political Editor *Douglas Fraser*
Sports Editor *David Dick*
Entertainment Editor *Andrew Burnet*
Magazine Editor *Jane Wright*

Sunday Mail
One Central Quay, Glasgow G3 8DA
☎ 0141 309 3000   Fax 0141 309 3587
Website www.sundaymail.co.uk

Owner *Trinity Mirror plc*
Editor *Allan Rennie*
Circulation 605,743

Popular Scottish Sunday tabloid.
News Editor *Jim Wilson*
Features Editor *Susie Cormack*
7Days: Weekly supplement. Editor *Liz Steele*
Mailsport Monthly: Monthly magazine. Editor *George Cheyne*

Sunday Mirror
1 Canada Square, Canary Wharf, London E14 5AP
☎ 020 7293 3000   Fax 020 7293 3939 (news desk)
Website www.sundaymirror.co.uk

Owner *Trinity Mirror*
Editor *Tina Weaver*
Circulation 1.6 million

In general terms contributions are welcome, though the paper patiently points out it has more time for those who have taken the trouble to study the market. Initial contact in writing preferred, except for live news situations. No fiction.
News Editor *James Scott* The news desk is very much in the market for tip-

offs and inside information. Contributors would be expected to work with staff writers on news stories. Approach by telephone or fax in the first instance.

Finance *Melanie Wright*

Features Editor *Nicky Dawson* 'Anyone who has obviously studied the market will be dealt with constructively and courteously.' Cherishes its record as a breeding ground for new talent.

Travel Editor *Gill Williams*

M Celebs: Colour supplement. Editor *Mel Brodie*

Sunday Post

2 Albert Square, Dundee DD1 9QJ

☎ 01382 223131   Fax 01382 201064

Email mail@sundaypost.com

Website www.sundaypost.com

Owner *D.C. Thomson & Co. Ltd*

Editor *David Pollington*

Circulation 530,168

Contributions should be addressed to the editor.

Sunday Post Magazine: Monthly colour supplement. Editor *Jan Gooderham*

Sunday Sport

19 Great Ancoats Street, Manchester M60 4BT

☎ 0161 236 4466   Fax 0161 236 4535

Website www.sundaysport.com

Owner *David Sullivan*

Editor *Paul Carter*

Circulation 178,740

FOUNDED 1986. Sunday tabloid catering for a particular sector of the male 15–35 readership. As concerned with 'glamour' (for which, read: 'page 3') as with human interest, news, features and sport. Unsolicited mss are welcome; receives about 90 a week. Approach should be made by phone in the case of news and sports items, by letter for features. All material should be addressed to the news editor.

News Editor *Nick Appleyardie* Off-beat news, human interest, preferably with photographs.

Showbiz Editor *Alice Walker* Regular items: showbiz, television, films, pop music and gossip.

Sports Editor *Marc Smith* Hard-hitting sports stories on major soccer clubs and their personalities, plus leading clubs/people in other sports. Strong quotations to back up the news angle essential.

PAYMENT negotiable and on publication.

The Sunday Telegraph

1 Canada Square, Canary Wharf, London E14 5DT

☎ 020 7538 5000   Fax 020 7538 6242

Website www.telegraph.co.uk

Owner *Conrad Black*
Editor *Dominic Lawson*
Circulation 697,771

Right-of-centre quality Sunday paper which, although traditionally formal, has pepped up its image to attract a younger readership. Unsolicited material from untried writers is rarely ever used. Contact with idea and details of track record.

News Editor *Richard Ellis*
Features Editor *Susannah Herbert*
City Editor *Robert Peston*
Political Editor *Patrick Hennessy*
Education Editor *Julie Henry*
Arts Editor *Lucy Tuck*
Environment Editor *David Harrison*
Literary Editor *Miriam Gross*
Diary Editor *Tim Walker*
Travel Editor *Graham Boynton*
Sunday Telegraph Magazine: Colour supplement. Editor *Anna Murphy*

The Sunday Times

1 Pennington Street, London E98 1ST
☎ 020 7782 5000   Fax 020 7782 5658
Website www.sunday-times.co.uk

Owner *News International plc/Rupert Murdoch*
Editor *John Witherow*
Circulation 1.4 million

FOUNDED 1820. Tendency to be anti-establishment, with a strong crusading investigative tradition. Approach the relevant editor with an idea in writing. Close scrutiny of the style of each section of the paper is strongly advised before sending mss. No fiction. All fees by negotiation.
News Editor *Charles Hymas* Opportunities are very rare.
News Review Editor *Eleanor Mills* Submissions are always welcome, but the paper commissions its own, uses staff writers or works with literary agents, by and large. The features sections where most opportunities exist are *Style* and *The Culture*.
Culture Editor *Helen Hawkins*
Business Editor *William Lewis*
City Editor *Paul Durman*
Education Editor *Geraldine Hackett*
Science/Environment *Jonathan Leake*
Literary Editor *Caroline Gascoigne*
Travel Editor *Christine Walker*
Style Editor *Tiffanie Darke*
Sunday Times Magazine: Colour supplement. Editor *Robin Morgan* No unsolicited material. Write with ideas in the first instance.
Sunday Times Travel Magazine: Monthly supplement. Editor *Jan Knight*

The Times

1 Pennington Street, London E98 1TT
☎ 020 7782 5000   Fax 020 7488 3242
Website www.thetimes.co.uk

Owner *News International plc/Rupert Murdoch*
Editor *Robert Thomson*
Circulation 658,637

Generally right (though features can range in tone from diehard to libertarian). *The Times* receives a great many unsolicited offerings. Writers with feature ideas should approach by letter in the first instance. No fiction.
Deputy Editor *Ben Preston*
News Editor *John Wellman*
Features Editor *Michael Harve*
Associate Editor *Brian MacArthur*
City/Financial Editor *Patience Wheatcroft*
Diary Editor *Andrew Pierce*
Arts Editor *Sarah Vine*
Literary Editor *Erica Wagner*
Travel Editor *Cath Urquhart*
Weekend Review Editor *Ben MacIntyre*
The Times Magazine: Saturday supplement. Editor *Gill Morgan*
Times 2: Editor *Sandra Parsons*

Magazines

Business Traveller
Nestor House, Playhouse Yard, London EC4V 5EX
☎ 020 7778 0000   Fax 020 7778 0022
Email editorial@businesstraveller.com
Website www.businesstraveller.com

Owner *Euromoney Institutional Investor Plc*
Editor-in-Chief *Tom Otley*
Circulation 500,000 (worldwide)

MONTHLY. Consumer publication. Opportunities exist for freelance writers but unsolicited contributions tend to be about leisure travel rather than business travel. Would-be contributors are strongly advised to study the magazine or the website first. Approach in writing with ideas. PAYMENT varies.

Co-op Traveller
Wrap Communications Ltd, The Bake House, J108 TBBC, 100 Clements Road, London SE16 4DG
☎ 020 7231 0707   Fax 020 7231 1232
Email info@wrapcom.com
Website www.wrapcom.com

Owner *United Co-op Travel Division/Wrap Communications*
Editor *Ciaran Jennings*
Circulation 150,000

FOUNDED 2001. BIANNUAL magazine for Co-op Travel customers. Travel articles and travel-related news for the independent traveller. No unsolicted material; approach by telephone, fax, letter or email in the first instance.
FEATURES Ideas for exciting travel features, including destinations, accommodation, activities etc. Maximum 1000 words.
News Stories that reveal fascinating facts for holidaymakers, including interesting products, new destinations and developments in the travel market. Maximum 300 words.
PAYMENT negotiable.

Condé Nast Traveller
Vogue House, Hanover Square, London w1s 1ju
☎ 020 7499 9080   Fax 020 7493 3758
Email editorcntraveller@condenast.co.uk
Website www.cntraveller.co.uk
Owner *Condé Nast Publications*
Editor *Sarah Miller*
Circulation 82,780

FOUNDED 1997. MONTHLY travel magazine. Proposals rather than completed mss preferred. Approach in writing in the first instance. No unsolicited photographs. 'The magazine has a no freebie policy and no writing can be accepted on the basis of a press or paid-for trip.'

House & Garden
Vogue House, Hanover Square, London w1s 1ju
☎ 020 7499 9080   Fax 020 7629 2907
Website www.condenast.co.uk
Owner *Condé Nast Publications Ltd*
Editor *Susan Crewe*
Circulation 148,716

FOUNDED 1947. MONTHLY. Most feature material is produced in-house but occasional specialist features are commissioned from qualified freelancers, mainly for the interiors, wine and food sections and travel.

FEATURES *Liz Elliot* Suggestions for features, preferably in the form of brief outlines of proposed subjects, will be considered.

In Britain

Jubilee House, 2 Jubilee Place, London sw3 3TQ

☎ 020 7751 4800   Fax 020 7751 4848

Email inbritain@romseypublishing.com

Editor *Andrea Spain*
Circulation 47,000

FOUNDED in the 1930s. BI-MONTHLY. Travel magazine of 'VisitBritain'. Not much opportunity for unsolicited work – approach (by email) with ideas and samples. Words and picture packages preferred (good quality transparencies only).

Loaded

IPC Media Ltd., King's Reach Tower, Stamford Street, London SE1 9LS

☎ 020 7261 5562   Fax 020 7261 5557

Email andrew_woods@ipcmedia.com

Owner *IPC Media*
Editor *Martin Daubney*
Features Editor *Andrew Woods*
Circulation 263,108

FOUNDED 1994. MONTHLY men's lifestyle magazine featuring music, sport, sex, humour, travel, fashion, hard news and popular culture. Will consider material which comes into these categories; approach the features editor in writing or by email in the first instance. No fiction or poetry.

Practical Caravan
60 Waldegrave Road, Teddington TW11 8LG
☎ 020 8267 5629   Fax 020 8267 5725
Email practical.caravan@haynet.com
Website www.practicalcaravan.com

Owner *Haymarket Magazines Ltd*
Editor *Alex Newby*
Circulation 41,665

FOUNDED 1967. MONTHLY. Contains caravan reviews, travel features, investigations, products, park reviews. Unsolicited mss welcome on travel relevant only to caravanning/touring vans. No motorcaravan or static van stories. Approach with ideas by phone, letter or email.
FEATURES Must refer to caravanning. Written in friendly, chatty manner. Pictures essential. Max. length 2000 words.
PAYMENT negotiable.

Safeway The Magazine
Redwood, 7 Saint Martin's Place, London WC2N 4HA
☎ 020 7747 0788   Fax 020 7747 0799

Editor *Jennifer Newton*
Circulation 1.8 million

FOUNDED 1996. MONTHLY in-store magazine covering food and recipes, beauty, health, shopping, gardens, travel and features. Regular freelancers are employed and although outside material is rarely used ideas will be considered for beauty, health, travel and features. Approach in writing in the first instance.

Tramp Magazine
South Bank House, Black Prince Road, London SE1 7SJ
☎ 020 7735 8171
Email info@trampmagazine.com
Website www.trampmagazine.com

Owner *Enrico Williams*
Editor *Kirsten Telfer-Beith*
Circulation 60,000

FOUNDED 2003. MONTHLY luxury lifestyle magazine. Travel, entertainment, lifestyle and fashion items welcome; approach by email.
TRAVEL *Christina Haynes*
FOOD *Malaika Aaron-Pereira*
LIFESTYLE *Paolla Steinhart-Smith*

Vogue

Vogue House, Hanover Square, London W1S 1JU
☎ 020 7499 9080   Fax 020 7408 0559
Website www.vogue.co.uk

Owner *Condé Nast Publications Ltd*
Editor *Alexandra Shulman*
Circulation 202,259

Condé Nast Magazines tend to use known writers and commission what's needed, rather than using unsolicited mss. Contacts are useful.
FEATURES *Jo Craven*. Upmarket general interest rather than 'women's'. Good proportion of highbrow art and literary articles, as well as travel, gardens, food, home interest and reviews.

Travel Writers' Association

British Guild of Travel Writers

12 Askew Crescent, London W12 9DW

☎ 020 8749 1128   Fax 020 8749 1128

Email charlotte.c@virtualnecessities.com

Website www.bgtw.org

Chairman *Melissa Shales*

Secretariat *Charlotte Copeman*

Subscription £100 p.a.

The professional association of travel writers, broadcasters, photographers and editors which aims to serve its members' professional interests by acting as a forum for debate, discussion and 'networking'. The Guild publishes an annual Year Book and has a website giving full details of all its members and useful trade contacts, holds monthly meetings and has a monthly newsletter. Members are required to spend a significant proportion of their working time on travel.

Arts Councils and Regional Offices

The Arts Council England
14 Great Peter Street, London SW1P 3NQ
☎ 020 7333 0100   Fax 020 7973 6564   Textphone 020 7973 6564
Email enquiries@artscouncil.org.uk
Website www.artscouncil.org.uk

Chairman *Professor Sir Christopher Frayling*
Chief Executive *Peter Hewitt*
Director of Literature *Gary McKeone*

Arts Council England is the national development agency for the arts in England, distributing public money from government and the National Lottery to artists and arts organisations. Arts Council England works independently and at arm's length from government. Information about Arts Council England funding is available on the website, by email or by contacting the enquiry line on 0845 300 6200.

Arts Council England has 9 regional offices:

Arts Council England, East
Eden House, 48–49 Bateman Street, Cambridge CB2 1LR
☎ 0845 300 6200   Fax 0870 242 1271   Textphone 01223 306893

Arts Council England, East Midlands
St Nicholas Court, 25–27 Castle Gate, Nottingham NG1 7AR
☎ 0845 300 6200   Fax 0115 950 2467

Arts Council England, London
2 Pear Tree Court, London EC1R 0DS
☎ 0845 300 6200   Fax 020 7608 4100 Textphone 020 7608 4101
Head of Literature *Nick McDowell*

Arts Council England, North East
Central Square, Forth Street, Newcastle upon Tyne NE1 3PJ
☎ 0845 300 6200   Fax 0191 230 1020 Textphone 0191 255 8500

Arts Council England, North West
Manchester House, 22 Bridge Street Manchester M3 3AB
☎ 0161 834 6644   Fax 0161 834 6969 Textphone 0161 834 9131

Arts Council England, South East
Sovereign House, Church Street, Brighton BN1 1RA
☎ 0845 300 6200   Fax 0870 242 1257 Textphone 01273 710659

Arts Council England, South West
Bradninch Place, Gandy Street, Exeter EX4 3LS
Tel 0845 300 6200   Fax 01392 229229 Textphone 01392 433503

Arts Council England, West Midlands
82 Granville Street, Birmingham B1 2LH
☎ 0845 300 6200   Fax 0121 643 7239 Textphone 0121 643 2815

Arts Council England, Yorkshire
21 Bond Street, Dewsbury WF13 1AX
☎ 0845 300 6200   Fax 01924 466522 Textphone 01924 438585

The Arts Council/An Chomhairle Ealaíon

70 Merrion Square, Dublin 2 Republic of Ireland
☎ 00 353 1 618 0200   Fax 00 353 1 676 1302
Email artistsservices@artscouncil.ie
Website www.artscouncil.ie

Director *Patricia Quinn*
Literature Specialist (English language) *Bronwen Williams*
Literature Specialist (Irish language) *Róisin Ní Mhianáin*
Artists' Services Manager *Paul Johnson*

The development agency for the arts in Ireland. An autonomous statutory body, appointed by the Irish government to promote and assist the arts. Established by the Arts Act of 1951. In fulfilling its remit, the Council provides advice to the Irish government on artistic matters; advice, assistance and support to individuals, arts organisations and a wide range of governmental and non-governmental bodies; and financial assistance to individuals and organisations for artistic purposes. The Council also part funds county and city arts officers throughout the country. It consists of 12 members and a chair appointed by the Minister for Arts, Sport and Tourism for a period of not more than five years. Its state grant in 2004 was $52.5 million.

Of particular interest to individual writes is the Council's free booklet, *Support for Artists*, which describes bursaries, awards and schemes on offer and how to apply for them. Applicants to these awards must be of Irish birth or resident in Ireland.

The Arts Council of Northern Ireland

MacNeice House, 77 Malone Road, Belfast BT9 6AQ
☎ 028 9038 5200   Fax 028 9066 1715
Email rmeredith@artscouncil-ni.org
Website www.artscouncil-ni.org

Literature and Language Arts Officer *Robbie Meredith*

Funds book production by established publishers, programmes of readings, literary festivals, writers-in-residence schemes and literary magazines and periodicals. Occasional schools' programmes and anthologies of children's writing are produced. Annual awards and bursaries for writers are available. Holds information also on various groups associated with local arts, workshops and courses.

Scottish Arts Council

12 Manor Place, Edinburgh EH3 7DD
☎ 0131 226 6051   Fax 0131 225 9833
Email administrator@scottisharts.org.uk
Website www.scottisharts.org.uk

Chairman *James Boyle*
Director *Graham Berry*
Head of Literature *Gavin Wallace*
Literature Officers *Jenny Attala, Sophy Dale*
Literature Secretary *Catherine Allen*

Principal channel for government funding of the arts in Scotland. The Scottish Arts Council (SAC) is funded by the Scottish Executive. It aims to develop and improve the knowledge, understanding and practice of the arts, and to increase their accessibility throughout Scotland. It offers around 1300 grants a year to artists and arts organisations concerned with the visual arts, crafts, dance and mime, drama, literature, music, festivals and traditional, ethnic and community arts. It is also a distributor of National Lottery funds to the arts in Scotland. SAC's support for Scottish-based writers with a track record of publication includes bursaries, writing fellowships and book awards. Information offered includes lists of literature awards, literary magazines, agents and publishers.

The Arts Council of Wales

Museum Place, Cardiff CF10 3NX
☎ 029 2037 6500   Fax 029 2022 1447
Website www.artswales.org

Senior Officer: Drama *Sandra Wynne*

In April 2003 the responsibility for funding literary magazines and book production transferred to the Welsh Books Council. Services for individual writers including bursaries, mentoring, the critical writers service and writers in residency/writers on tour are provided by the Welsh Academy, Hay-on-Wye Literature Festival and Ty Newydd Writers' Centre at Cricieth. The Council aims to develop theatrical experience among Wales-based writers through a variety of schemes – in particular, by funding writers on year-long attachments.

Writers' Courses and Workshops

England

Berkshire

University of Reading
The School of Continuing Education, London Road, Reading
RG1 5AQ
☎ 0118 378 8347
Email Cont-Ed@reading.ac.uk
Website www.reading.ac.uk/ContEd

An expanding programme of creative writing courses, including *Life into Fiction*; *Poetry Workshop*; *Getting Started*; *Writing Fiction*; *Publishing Poetry*; *Scriptwriting*; *Travel Writing*; *Comedy Writing* and *Writing for Radio*. There is also a public lecture by a writer and a reading by students of their work, and various Saturday workshops. Tutors include novelist Leslie Wilson and poets Jane Draycott, Elizabeth James and Susan Utting, David Grubb and Paul Bavister. Fees vary depending on the length of course. Concessions available.

Buckinghamshire

Missenden Abbey Adult Learning

Great Missenden HP16 OBD

☎ 0845 045 4040   Fax 01753 783756

Email adultlearningchil@buckscc.gov.uk

Website www.aredu.org.uk/missendenabbey

Residential and non-residential weekend workshops, Easter and summer school. Programmes have included *Writing Stories for Children*; *Short Story Writing*; *Poetry Workshop*; *Writing for TV and Film*; *Writing Comedy for Television*; *Life Writing*; *Travel Tales*.

Yorkshire

University of Sheffield

Institute for Lifelong Learning, 196–198 West Street, Sheffield S1 4ET

☎ 0114 222 7000   Fax 0114 222 7001

Website www.shef.ac.uk/till

Certificate in *Creative Writing* (Degree Level 1) and a wide range of courses, from foundation level to specialist writing areas, open to all. Courses in poetry, prose, journalism, scriptwriting, comedy, travel writing, writing using ICT/Web, writing for children. Brochures and information available from the address above.

Bursaries and Prizes

The BBCFour Samuel Johnson Prize for Non-Fiction
Colman Getty PR, Middlesex House, 34–42 Cleveland Street, London W1T 4JE
☎ 020 7631 2666   Fax 020 7631 2699
Email cathryn@colmangettypr.co.uk

Contact *Cathryn Summerhayes*

Established 1998. Annual prize sponsored by BBCFour. Eligible categories include the arts, autobiography, biography, business, commerce, current affairs, history, natural history, popular science, religion, sport and travel. Entries submitted by publishers only. 2003 winner: Tim Binyon *Pushkin*. PRIZE £30,000; £1000 to each shortlisted author.

The Thomas Cook Travel Book Award
Thomas Cook Publishing, PO Box 227, Peterborough PE3 8XX
☎ 01733 417352   Fax 01733 416688

Established in 1980 by The Thomas Cook Group. Annual award given to the author of the book, published (in the English language) in the previous year, which most inspires the reader to want to travel. Submissions by publishers only. 2003 winner: Jenny Diski *Stranger on a Train*. AWARD £10,000.

Somerset Maugham Trust Fund

The Society of Authors, 84 Drayton Gardens, London SW10 9SB

☎020 7373 6642   Fax 020 7373 5768

Email info@societyofauthors.org

Website www.societyofauthors.org

Annual awards designed to encourage writers under the age of 35 to travel. Given on the basis of a published work of fiction, non-fiction or poetry. Open only to British-born subjects resident in the UK. Final entry date: 20 December. 2003 winners: Hari Kunzru *The Impressionist*; William Fiennes *The Snow Geese*; Jon McGregor *If Nobody Speaks of Remarkable Things*. AWARDS £12,000 (total).

WHSmith's 'People's Choice' Book Awards

WHSmith PLC, Nations House, 103 Wigmore Street, London W1U 1WH

☎020 7514 9623   Fax 020 7514 9635

Email elizabeth.walker@WHSmith.co.uk

Website www.WHSmithbookawards.co.uk

Contact *Elizabeth Walker, Group Event Marketing Manager*

Now in their fourth year, these WHSmith book awards were the first where the winners are voted for entirely by the public. Teams of celebrity and public judges choose the shortlists but *any* book published during the calendar year can be voted for. There are nine award categories in total. Eight are voted for by the public: Fiction; Debut Novel; Lifestyle; Autobiography/Biography; Travel Writing; Business; Factual and Teen Choice. Voting (in any WHSmith store, local library, by text message, freepost or via the website) starts in January (lasting six weeks) and winners are announced in March. Recent winners have included Jamie Oliver, Ben Elton, Sir David Attenborough and Donna Tartt. The ninth category, the long-standing WHSmith Literary Award, is not put out to public vote but is decided by a panel led by the Professor of English Literature at Merton College, Oxford, and Chief Book Reviewer for the *Sunday Times*, John Carey. Three members of the public join at shortlist stage to help decide the winner.

PRIZES Each winning author receives a trophy and £5000.

The Travelling Scholarships

The Society of Authors, 84 Drayton Gardens, London SW10 9SB

☎ 020 7373 6642   Fax 020 7373 5768

Email info@societyofauthors.org

Website www.societyofauthors.org

Annual honorary grants to established British writers. 2003 winners: Kate Chisolm, Jamie McKendrick, Aonghas MacNeacail.

AWARD £6000 (total).

Library Services

Bromley House Library
Angel Row, Nottingham NG1 6HL
☎ 0115 947 3134

Librarian *Julia Wilson*
OPEN 9.30 am to 5.00 pm Monday to Friday; also first Saturday of each month from 10.00 am to 12.30 pm
ACCESS For members only

FOUNDED 1816 as the Nottingham Subscription Library. Collection of 30,000 books including local history, topography, biography, travel and fiction.

The London Library
14 St James's Square, London SW1Y 4LG
☎ 020 7930 7705   Fax 020 7766 4766
Email membership@londonlibrary.co.uk
Website www.londonlibrary.co.uk

Librarian *Miss Inez Lynn*
OPEN 9.30 am to 5.30 pm Monday, Friday, Saturday; 9.30 am to 7.30 pm Tuesday, Wednesday, Thursday
ACCESS For members only (£170 p.a., 2004)

With over a million books and 8400 members, The London Library 'is the most distinguished private library in the world; probably the largest, certainly the best loved'. FOUNDED in 1841, it is a registered charity and wholly independent of public funding. Its permanent collection embraces most European languages as well as English. Its subject range is predominantly within the humanities, with emphasis on literature, history, fine and applied art, architecture, bibliography, philosophy, religion, and topography and travel. Some 8000–9000 titles are added yearly. Most of the stock is on open shelves to which members have free access. Members may take out up to 10 volumes; 15 if they live more than 20 miles from the Library. The comfortable Reading Room has an annexe for users of personal computers. There are photocopiers, CD-ROM workstations, free access to the Internet, and the Library also offers a postal loans service.

Prospective members are required to submit a refereed application form in advance of admission, but there is at present no waiting list for membership. The London Library Trust may make grants to those who are unable to afford the full annual fee; details on application.

Picture Libraries

Aviation Picture Library
116 The Avenue, St Stephens, West Ealing, London W13 8JX
☎ 020 8566 7712 (Mobile 07860 670073)   Fax 020 8566 7714
Email avpix@aol.com
Website www.aviationpictures.com

Contact *Austin John Brown*

Specialists in the aviation field but also a general library which includes travel, architecture, transport, landscapes and skyscapes. Special collections Aircraft and all aspects of the aviation industry, including the archival collection of John Stroud; aerial obliques of Europe, USA, Caribbean and West Africa; architectural and town planning. Photographers for *Flyer* magazine in the UK. Commissions undertaken on the ground and in the air.

Hamish Brown MBE, D.Litt, FRSGS Scottish Photographic
26 Kirkcaldy Road, Burntisland KY3 9HQ
☎ 01592 873546

Contact *Hamish Brown*

Coverage of most topics and areas of Scotland (sites, historic buildings, landscape, mountains), also travel, mountains, general (50,000 items) and Morocco. Commissions undertaken.

Christel Clear Marine Photography

5 Providence Place, Stoke Damerel, Plymouth PL1 5QS

☎ 01752 297598   Fax 07931 157717

Email julianne@cristelclear.co.uk

Website www.cristelclear.co.uk

Contact *Julie-Anne Wilce*

Over 70,000 images on 35mm and 645 transparencies: yachting and boating from Grand Prix sailing to small dinghies, cruising locations and harbours. Recent additions include angling, fly fishing and travel. Visitors by appointment.

Chrysalis Images

The Chrysalis Building, Bramley Road, London W10 6SP

☎ 020 7314 1400   Fax 020 7314 1583

Email pictures@chrysalisbooks.co.uk

Contact *Terry Forshaw*

One million photographs and illustrations, colour and b&w, on military, history, transport, cookery, crafts, natural history, space and travel.

John Cleare/Mountain Camera

Hill Cottage, Fonthill Gifford, Salisbury SP3 6QW

☎ 01747 820320   Fax 01747 820320

Email cleare@btinternet.com

Website www.mountaincamera.com

Colour and b&w coverage of mountains and wild places, climbing, ski-touring, trekking, expeditions, wilderness travel, landscapes, people and geographical features from all continents. Specialises in the Himalaya, Andes, Antarctic, Alps and the British countryside, and a range of topics from reindeer in Lapland to camels in Australia, from whitewater rafting in Utah to ski-mountaineering in China. Commissions and consultancy work undertaken. Researchers welcome by appointment. Member of **BAPLA** and the **OWG**.

Sylvia Cordaiy Photo Library
45 Rotherstone, Devizes SN10 2DD
☎ 01380 728327   Fax 01380 728328
Email info@sylvia-cordaiy.com
Website www.sylvia-cordaiy.com

Over 170 countries on file from the obscure to main stock images – Africa, North, Central and South America, Asia, Atlantic, Indian and Pacific Ocean islands, Australasia, Europe, polar regions. Covers travel, architecture, ancient civilisations, people worldwide, environment, wildlife, natural history, Antarctica, domestic pets, livestock, marine biology, veterinary treatment, equestrian, ornithology, flowers. UK files cover cities, towns, villages, coastal and rural scenes, London collection. Transport, railways, shipping and aircraft (military and civilian). Aerial photography. Backgrounds and abstracts. Also the Paul Kaye B/W archive.

Philip Craven Worldwide Photo-Library
Surrey Studios, 21 Nork Way, Nork, Banstead SM7 1PB
☎ 0870 220 2121
Website www.philipcraven.com

Contact *Philip Craven*

Extensive coverage of British scenes, cities, villages, English countryside, gardens, historic buildings and wildlife. Worldwide travel and wildlife subjects on medium- and large-format transparencies.

James Davis Worldwide
65 Brighton Road, Shoreham BN43 6RE
☎ 01273 452252   Fax 01273 440116
Email library@eyeubiquitous.com
Website www.eyeubiquitous.com

Travel collection: people, places, emotive scenes and tourism. Constantly updated by a team of photographers, both at home and abroad. Same-day service available.

Exile Images

1 Mill Row, West Hill Road, Brighton BN1 3SU

☎ 01273 208741   Fax 01273 382782

Email pics@exileimages.co.uk

Website www.exileimages.co.uk

Contact *Howard Davies*

Online photo library with over 5000 pictures of refugees, conflict, asylum seekers, UK protests and Third World issues. Picture editors can search and download high resolution photographs online.

ffotograff

10 Kyveilog Street, Pontcanna, Cardiff CF11 9JA

☎ 029 2023 6879

Email ffotograff@easynet.co.uk

Website www.ffotograff.com

Contact *Patricia Aithie*

Library and agency specialising in travel, exploration, the arts, architecture, traditional culture, archaeology and landscape. Based in Wales but specialising in the Middle and Far East; Africa, Central and South America; Yemen and Wales are strong aspects of the library. Churches and cathedrals of Britain and Crusader castles.

Andrew N. Gagg's Photo Flora

Town House Two, Fordbank Court, Henwick Road, Worcester WR2 5PF

☎ 01905 748515

Email a.n.gagg@ntlworld.com

Website homepage.ntlworld.com/a.n.gagg/photo/photoflora.html

Specialist in British and European wild plants, flowers, ferns, grasses, trees, shrubs, etc. with colour coverage of most British and many European species (rare and common) and habitats; also travel in India, Sri Lanka, Nepal, Egypt, China, Mexico, Thailand, Tibet, Vietnam and Cambodia.

John Heseltine Archive

Mill Studio, Frogmarsh Mill, South Woodchester GL5 5ET

☎ 01453 873792

Email john@heseltine.co.uk

Website www.heseltine.co.uk

Contact *John Heseltine*

Over 200,000 colour transparencies and digital files of landscapes, architecture, food and travel with particular emphasis on Italy and the UK.

Chris Howes/Wild Places Photography

51 Timbers Square, Cardiff CF24 3SH

☎ 029 2048 6557   Fax 029 2048 6557

Email photos@wildplaces.co.uk

Contacts *Chris Howes, Judith Calford*

Expanding collection of over 50,000 colour transparencies and b&w prints covering travel, topography and natural history worldwide, plus action sports such as climbing. Specialist areas include caves, caving and mines (with historical coverage using engravings and early photographs), wildlife, landscapes and the environment, including pollution and conservation. Europe (including Britain), USA, Africa and Australia are all well represented within the collection. Commissions undertaken.

Illustrated London News Picture Library

20 Upper Ground, London SE1 9PF

☎ 020 7805 5585   Fax 020 7805 5905

Email iln.pictures@ilng.co.uk

Website www.ilnpictures.co.uk

Engravings, photographs and illustrations from 1842 to the present day, taken from magazines published by Illustrated Newspapers: *Illustrated London News*; *Graphic*; *Sphere*; *Tatler*; *Sketch*; *Illustrated Sporting and Dramatic News*; *Illustrated War News 1914–18*; *Bystander*; *Britannia & Eve*. Social history, London, Industrial Revolution, wars, travel. Visitors by appointment.

International Photobank

Unit D1, Roman Hill Business Park, Broadmayne DT2 8LY

☎ 01305 854145   Fax 01305 853065

Email peter@internationalphotobank.co.uk

Website www.internationalphotobank.co.uk

Over 400,000 transparencies, partly medium-format. Colour coverage of travel subjects: places, people, folklore, events. Assignments undertaken for guide books. ISDN digital service available for newspapers, magazines and other users.

André Laubier Picture Library

Flat 2, 1 Bishops Road, London N6 4HP

☎ 020 8341 2947

An extensive library of photographs from 1935 to the present day in 35mm and medium-format. Main subjects are: archaeology and architecture, art and artists (wood carving, sculptures, contemporary glass), botany, historical buildings, sites and events, landscapes, nature, leisure sports, events, experimental artwork and photography, people and travel. Substantial stock of many other subjects including: birds, buildings and cities, folklore, food and drink, gardens, transport. Special collection: Images d'Europe (Austria, Britain, France, Greece, S.W. Ireland, Italy, Spain, Turkey, Egypt – from

Cairo to Abu Simbel, Norway and former Yugoslavia). Africa and Kenyan safari. Private collection: World War II to D-Day. List available on request. Correspondence welcome in English, French or German.

Pictures Colour Library
10 James Whatman Court, Turkey Mill, Ashford Road, Maidstone
ME14 5SS
☎ 01622 609809   Fax 01622 609806
Email Researcher@PicturesColourLibrary.co.uk
Website www.picturescolourlibrary.co.uk

Travel and travel-related images depicting lifestyles and cultures, people and places, attitudes and environments from around the world, including a comprehensive section on Great Britain.

PPL (Photo Agency) Ltd
Bookers Yard, The Street, Walberton, Arundel BN18 0PF
☎ 01243 555561   Fax 01243 555562
Email ppl@mistral.co.uk
Website www.pplmedia.com
Contacts *Barry Pickthall, Natasha Wakefield*

Two million pictures covering watersports, sub-aqua, business and commerce, travel and tourism and a fast growing archive on Sussex and the home counties. Pictures available in high resolution directly from website.

Royal Geographical Society Picture Library
1 Kensington Gore, London SW7 2AR
☎ 020 7591 3060   Fax 020 7591 3061
Email pictures@rgs.org
Website www.rgs.org/picturelibrary
Contact *Justin Hobson*

A strong source of geographical and historical images, both archival and modern, showing the world through the eyes of photographers and explorers dating from the 1830s to the present day. The RGS Contemporary Collection provides up-to-date transparencies from around the world, highlighting aspects of cultural activity, environmental phenomena, anthropology, architectural design, travel, mountaineering and exploration. Offers a professional and comprehensive service for both commercial and academic use.

Skishoot – Offshoot
Hall Place, Upper Woodcott, Whitchurch RG28 7PY
☎ 01635 255527   Fax 01635 255528
Email skishootsnow@aol.com
Website www.skishoot.co.uk

Contacts *Kate Parker, Jo Crossley*

Skishoot ski and snowboarding picture library has 400,000 images. Offshoot travel library specialises in France.

SOA Photo Library
Lovells Farm, Dark Lane, Stoke St Gregory, Taunton TA3 6EU
☎ 0870 333 6062   Fax 0870 333 6082
Email info@soaphotoagency.com
Website www.soaphotoagency.com

Contact *Sabine Oppenlander*

85,000 colour slides, 15,000 b&w photos covering *Stern* productions, sports, travel and geographic, advertising, social subjects and funny photos. Representatives of Voller Ernst, Picture Press, Look and many freelance photographers. Free catalogues available.

Tessa Traeger Picture Library
7 Rossetti Studios, 72 Flood Street, London SW3 5TF
☎ 020 7352 3641   Fax 020 7352 4846

Email tessatraeger@solutions-inc.co.uk
Website www.tessatraeger.com

Food, gardens, travel and artists.

Travel Ink Photo & Feature Library

The Old Coach House, 14 High Street, Goring on Thames, Nr
Reading RG8 9AR
☎ 01491 873011   Fax 01491 875558
Email info@travel-ink.co.uk
Website www.travel-ink.co.uk

Contact *Felicity Bazell*

A collection of over 120,000 travel, tourism and lifestyle images, carefully
edited and constantly updated, from countries worldwide. Specialist collections from the UK, Greece, France, Hong Kong, Far East, Canada, USA and
Caribbean. The website offers a fully captioned and searchable selection of
over 20,000 images and is ideal for picture researchers.

World Pictures

25 Gosfield Street, London W1W 6HQ
☎ 020 7437 2121/7436 0440   Fax 020 7439 1307
Email worldpictures@btinternet.com
Website www.worldpictures.co.uk

Contacts *David Brenes, Carlo Irek*

600,000 colour transparencies of travel and emotive material.

The John Robert Young Collection

61 De Montfort Road, Lewes BN7 1SS
☎ 01273 475216   Fax 01273 475216
Email johnrobert@pxvobiscum.fsnet.co.uk
johnrobertyoung.members.beeb.net

Contact *Jennifer Barrett*

50,000 transparencies and monochrome prints on religion, travel and military subjects. Major portfolios: religious communities; the French Foreign Legion; the Spanish Legion; the Royal Marines; the People's Liberation Army (China).